Enjoy! JoAnna M. Lund

HEALTHY EXCHANGES®

JoAnna Lund's "Original" collection
of delicious "common folk" healthy recipes
created with the weight conscious,
heart patient and diabetic in mind . . .
but, oh so good, the entire family will enjoy!

CELERY

by
JoAnna M. Lund

Diabetic Calculations by Rose Hoenig, R.D., L.D.

Revised Dietary Calculated Edition - 1994

Art layout by Rebecca Dierickx Pelletier & Judy McNamara

DEDICATION

This book is dedicated to Barb, Carol,
Stephanie and Carol, my first "official tasting
team"; to my friend Shirley for typing,
retyping and then typing again;
and to my family, especially my
husband, Clifford, for much needed
support during this project.

Forward

You will be happy to see that this original HEALTHY EXCHANGES Cookbook has been revised so that all recipes provide complete nutrient information, just as does its successor, BEST OF HEALTHY EXCHANGES '92 Cookbook. Now both cookbooks provide flexibility in meal planning for folks interested in weight loss, fat and cholesterol reduction or diabetes management.

You can easily use these recipes as part of a total healthy diet with the addition of fruits, vegetables, milk, starches and lean proteins as needed. Eating for good health doesn't have to be the same old "diet foods". Any of these recipes will easily fit into your recommended meal plan.

Healthy Exchanges can be your guide to taking control of your eating habits and beginning a new 'Way of Life".

Rose Hoenig, RD, LD

ABOUT THE AUTHOR AND THE DIETITIAN

JoAnna Lund made a mid life career change from Commercial Insurance Underwriter to recipe developer when she was handed a burden she could not solve with cake donuts (three children involved in the Persian Gulf War). At her all time high weight of around 300 pounds with 56 inch hips, she knew she had to get healthy to handle the stress of the situation. Cake donuts were not going to keep her children safe. JoAnna had been a **professional dieter** for almost 30 years. She vowed to never diet again. Instead she put her energies into finding a workable solution both she and her truck drivin' man Cliff could live with. In the process she created a new career as publisher for both herself and her husband. JoAnna is a graduate of the University of Western Illinois, Macomb, IL. She is a member of the International Association of Culinary Professionals, Society for Nutrition Education; National Federation of Press Women; Newspaper Food Editors and Writers Association; Mid America Publishers Association and National Association of Independent Publishers. JoAnna and Cliff live in DeWitt, IA. They are the parents of three children, Becky Pelletier, James and Tom Dierickx, and are blessed with two wonderful children-in-law, Matt, husband of Becky and Pam, wife of James. In addition, the newest official taste tester is their grandson Zachary, son of James and Pam.

Rose Hoenig, RD,LD is a licensed, registered dietitian practicing in the Quad Cities. She is a graduate of Marycrest College, Davenport, IA and a member of the American Dietetic Association, Iowa Dietetic Association and President-elect of the Mississippi Valley Dietetic Association. She is also a member of the Iowa Consulting Dietitians in Health Care Facilities. Rose provides nutrition counseling to physicians and for various health care facilities. She and her husband Tony, live in Bettendorf, IA and have three children, Doug, Dan and Becky.

TABLE OF CONTENTS

In Loving Memory

To my parents, Jerome and Agnes McAndrews, who bestowed on me their earthly talents. I am indebted to my mother for my artistic approach to creating recipes and to my father for the analytical skills involved in having the exchanges come out right even when using the whole can!

I want to share the last poem my mother wrote, just days before she died to join my father in Heaven. I often wonder if she knew how comforting the last words she composed would be to me. I hope this poem comforts you as well.

I KNOW

I know there is a God, because

I feel His presence everywhere.

I know there is a God, for

He has taken me in His care.

Sometimes I doubt Him,

When I think my prayers go unheard,

Yet, I know He is aware of what

I am praying for, every single word.

He answers in His own way

According to His will.

So, I place my worries in His hands

And tell my heart be still.

Agnes Carrington McAndrews - 1990

JoAnna M. Lund once led her life as wife, mother of three, and Commercial Insurance Underwriter of 20 years, handling her stress quite well...by eating! She was overweight and unhappy, but not quite ready to force herself into a lifestyle change.

Then came the build-up for the Persian Gulf War. First, her son-in-law, Matt, a Green Beret, was restationed to Saudi Arabia, followed by his wife, JoAnna's daughter Becky, who was called to Active Army Reserves hospital duty in Germany. Unbelievably, on New Year's Eve, her son James was activated over the phone from Inactive Ready Reserves, receiving his orders by FAX.

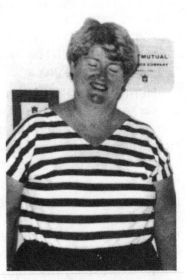

JoAnna's past history would have shown that under this extra-ordinary stress, she would have crumbled to eating whatever was "loose". Instead she prayed to God for strength, started walking regularly, joined a weight loss support group, and began a low sugar, low fat eating program.

Her quest for "diet food"- good-tasting, "common-people" dishes - led her to start experimenting with, testing and developing all types of recipes.

"I don't profess to be an expert or a nutritionist. I just figure common-sense ways to modify fat and sugar."

JoAnna started with a small amount of "real people food" to keep the flavor of the original recipe, while she worked to eliminate the excess fats and sugars, "making over" traditional recipes, as well as creating new ones. In the process she created a **method of success.**

Each recipe must fit all four of these guidelines to receive her approval:

1. low in fat, sugar and reasonably low sodium
2. easy to prepare
3. satisfying and have eye appeal
4. ingredients must be simple and easily found in the neighborhood grocery.

Her months of steady work in her small kitchen, using co-workers and family as "healthy food testers", led her to compiling an assortment of recipes into her first cookbook. HEALTHY EXCHANGES was published in October 1991.

In January of 1992, HEALTHY EXCHANGES Newsletter, a monthly publication with an average of 25+ new recipes, makeovers, ideas, and a complete meal, made its debut; followed in February by a Saturday morning call-in show on WOC 1420AM, Davenport, IA radio. JoAnna's husband/trucker, Cliff, joins her on the show, expressing his enjoyment of the taste testing of these new diet foods, especially the Triple Layer Party Pie! JoAnna also shares her healthy ideas through speaking presentations as well as monthly "low fat chef" segments on WQAD TV-8. She is a guest on call-in radio shows across the country weekly.

As of January 1993, all HE recipes offer the *dietary info for (1) Weight Loss Exchanges, (2) calories with grams and (3) Diabetic Exchanges.* HE is believed to be the first to offer this type of nutrient information.

In July of 1993, her second cookbook, "Best of Healthy Exchanges Newsletter '92", was published. She says one of the most frequent comments she receives after someone subscribes to the newsletter is "I just didn't believe I'd get this many recipes the family would enjoy!

Can I get the back issues?" So she combined the reader's favorite newsletter recipes of '92 into a cookbook. She says she has so many ideas to share in future cookbooks that it will be several years before she again uses the newsletter recipes to compile a cookbook.

"It's Not A Diet, It's A Way of Life"™ is a phrase that has become a slogan for HEALTHY EXCHANGES. It truly tells the story of JoAnna Lund. By January of 1994, just 36 months after taking James to the airport to leave for the Persian Gulf, she's left 130+ pounds behind her in her *"other"* lifestyle. HEALTHY EXCHANGES is a new way of life, not only in her body and emotional well-being, but also in her work. It's become a full-time job; the creating, marketing, correspondence and mailing of HEALTHY EXCHANGES products have become much more than *"a little kitchen hobby"* to make her diet food more desirable.

She says of her love of creating recipes, *"When life handed me a lemon, not only did I make healthy, tasty lemonade, I wrote the recipe down!"*

9

HEALTHY EXCHANGES
STANDARD RECIPE LEGEND

The Diabetic Exchanges are calculated by a Registered Dietitian and the other calculations are computer based.

The following symbols are used after each recipe.

SM = Milk	Ve = Vegetable
Fa = Fat	Pr = Protein
Br = Bread	Fr = Fruit
Sl = Slider	OC = Optional Calories
St = Starch	Mt = Meat
Ca = Carbohydrate	So = Sodium

These symbols will be used for all Weight Loss Exchanges (HEALTHY EXCHANGES); Grams (gm); Diabetic Exchanges listed .

For additional information about
HEALTHY EXCHANGES/Weight Loss Exchanges,
refer to pages **11** through **15** in this book
for extensive explanation.

Should you need additional information,
please feel free to call
319-659-8234

Before using these or any other collection of nutritional recipes, consult your physician or health provider to be sure they are appropriate for you. The information in this book is not intended to take the place of any medical advice. It reflects the author's experiences, studies, research, and opinions regarding healthy eating. All material included in this publication is believed to be accurate. The Publisher assumes no responsibility for any health, welfare or subsequent damage that might be incurred from use of these materials.

HEALTHY EXCHANGES WEIGHT LOSS EXCHANGES

Most of you using this book are already familiar with food exchanges. You can skip this part and begin using and enjoying the recipes, counting them towards your daily totals.

And for those of you who want to use the recipes because they are low fat and low sugar and are not concerned about exchanges, just prepare the recipes. Don't worry about the information on the bottom of each recipe.

However, if you are curious about the exchange system concept of eating, the following will give you a brief overview.

The idea is to divide foods into basic food groups. The foods found in each group are comparable in nutritional and caloric values. The food groups include Proteins, Breads, Vegetables, Fats, Fruits, Milk, Free Foods and Optional Calories.

If you want to lose weight, you should consult your physician or other weight control expert regarding the number of servings that would be best for YOU from each food group. Since men require more exchanges than women and children's requirements are different from adults, you can see the desired number of exchanges for any one person is a personal decision.

And as always, if you are a diabetic or have heart problems, it is best to visit with your physician before using this or any other food program or recipe collection.

PROTEINS

The foods in the Protein group include meat, poultry, seafood, eggs, cheese and legumes.

Examples of 1 protein exchange:

   1 oz of cooked weight meat, poultry or seafood

   1 egg

   3/4 oz cheese

   1/3 cup low fat cottage cheese
      or 1/2 cup fat free cottage cheese

   2 oz cooked or 3/4 oz uncooked dry beans

1 exchange of Protein is approximately 70 calories

BREADS

The foods in the Bread group include breads, crackers, cereals, grains and starchy vegetables.

Examples of 1 bread exchange:

   1 slice bread or 2 slices reduced calorie bread
      (40 calories or less)

   1/2 cup cooked pasta or rice

   3 Tablespoons flour

   3/4 oz cereal

   1/2 cup corn or peas

1 exchange of Bread is approximately 80 calories

FRUITS

The foods in the Fruit group include all fruits and fruit juices.

Examples of 1 fruit exchange:

> 1 small apple
>
> 1 small orange
>
> 1/2 medium banana
>
> 3/4 cup berries, except strawberries and cranberries which is 1 cup
>
> 1/2 cup canned fruit, packed in fruit juice
>
> 2 Tablespoons Raisins

1 exchange of Fruit is approximately 60 calories

MILK

The foods in the Milk group include milk, buttermilk and yogurt.

Examples of 1 milk exchange:

> 1 cup skim milk
>
> 1/2 cup evaporated skim milk
>
> 1 cup low fat buttermilk
>
> 1/2 cup low fat plain yogurt
> or 3/4 cup plain fat free yogurt
>
> 1/3 cup dry skim milk powder

1 exchange of Milk is approximately 90 calories

13

VEGETABLE

The foods included in the Vegetable group are all vegetables other than the starchy vegetables. This includes fresh, canned or frozen vegetables.

   1/2 cup of a vegetable equals 1 exchange

1 exchange of Vegetables is approximately 30 calories

FATS

The foods in the Fat group include margarine, mayonnaise, vegetable oils, salad dressings, olives and nuts.

Examples of 1 fat exchange:

   1 teaspoon margarine or 2 teaspoons
      reduced calorie margarine

   1 teaspoon vegetable oil

   1 teaspoon mayonnaise or 2 teaspoons
      reduced calorie mayonnaise

   1 teaspoon peanut butter

   1 oz olives

   1/4 oz pecans

1 exchange of Fat is approximately 40 calories

14

FREE FOODS

Foods that don't provide nutritional value, but are used to enhance the taste are included in the Free Foods. Examples are spices, herbs, extracts, vinegar, lemon juice, mustard, Worcestershire sauce and Soy sauce. Cooking sprays and artificial sweeteners used in moderation are also included in this group. However, I included the caloric value of artificial sweeteners in the optional calories breakdown of the recipes.

OPTIONAL CALORIES

Foods that don't fit into any other group, but are used in moderation in recipes are included in optional calories. Examples are sugar free gelatin and puddings, no fat mayonnaise and dressings, reduced calorie whipped toppings, reduced calorie syrups and jams, chocolate chips, coconut and canned broth.

SLIDERS

These are 80 optional calorie increments, that do not fall into any particular category. You can choose your own food group to *slide* it into. It is wise to limit this selection to 2 or 3 times a week to insure the best possible nutrition for your body while still enjoying an occasional treat.

HEALTHY EXCHANGES AND SPECIAL DIETS

By Rose Hoenig, RD, LD

The recipes in Healthy Exchanges are designed to be low in fats and sugars. This makes them very useful for persons with diabetes, heart disease or for anyone trying to eat a healthier diet. Sugar substitutes are regularly used as well as many new sugar free and low fat foods found in the local supermarket. The fat and cholesterol content of each recipe is quite low, with most recipes providing less than ten grams of fat per serving. Sodium content varies, so if you have been advised to eat less than 3000 grams of sodium per day, consult with your physician or dietitian for specific recommendations. Healthy Exchanges is intended to be used as a part of a total healthy diet with the addition of other foods to meet individual nutrient needs.

Meal planning for diabetics is based on six food groups called exchanges, published by the American Dietetic Association and The American Diabetes Association, Inc. The six groups or lists are: starch/bread, meat/protein, vegetables, fruit, milk and fat. Foods are grouped together in a list because they are alike. Every food on a list has about the same amount of carbohydrate, protein, fat and calories. Any food on a list can be exchanged or traded for any other food on the same list. These lists can be obtained from the American Diabetic Association or American Dietetic Association.

You may occasionally see a recipe that lists "free food" as part of the portion. According to the published exchange lists, a free food contains less than 20 calories per serving. Two or three servings per day of free foods/drinks is usually allowed in a meal plan.

Recipes can be calculated according to how the various ingredients fit into the six exchange lists. To simplify meal planning, exchanges less than one half are not used. This means that extra calories from various food groups may not be exactly accounted for. Generally, this will not cause a diabetic any problems unless a larger serving than the recipe gives is eaten. This is a noticeable difference from some weight loss programs.

16

If you are very familiar with diabetic exchanges and nutrient values of foods you may notice that amounts of carbohydrate, protein and fat given in a recipe portion do not always match what is listed in the published exchanges. This may be due to several reasons:

(1) As new foods reach the market they have been formed to be lower in fat. Sometimes small amounts of carbohydrate are added as thickeners or to add flavor and sweetness. These additions will alter the final nutrient value of that food.

(2) In some recipes there are parts of many food groups. In the exchange system portions less than 1/2 are usually not used. To simplify meal planning and to be as accurate as possible, the carbohydrate that is found in some foods may be counted as another group that also contains carbohydrate. For example, a recipe with a combination of vegetables and fruits may not contain enough of each food to equal at least 1/2 exchange but by combining the carbohydrate value of both foods the result is one whole serving of a fruit or vegetable. This method is used to help diabetics follow a typical meal plan that is developed to fit into their normal routine, without becoming too detailed.

(3) Recipes have been calculated using the diabetic exchanges and computerized nutrient analysis. Since the exchange lists are based on averages of food groups and the computer analysis is based on individual foods the total calories, carbohydrate, fat, and protein value of a recipe portion will not always match. In making a decision on what value to give a portion, this information is taken into account as well as how the average person would plan this food into their daily diet. A good recipe will provide a reasonable portion from an exchange group that would normally be eaten at a meal. One goal of diabetic meal planning is to provide flexibility, while keeping calories and carbohydrate fairly consistent. If your meal plan does not have enough exchanges to allow for the portion given, try using half the portion listed on the recipe. It is a good idea to check with your nutrition counselor before you change your meal plan.

17

USEFUL TIPS AND TIDBITS
FROM
HEALTHY EXCHANGES

January of 1991 I decided to "get serious" about living a healthier lifestyle. I had extreme external stress I could not change, and knew I had to be in better physical shape to cope. So, I began a **daily walking routine** and a **sensible eating program**. I limited my **intake of fats** and **processed sugars**. I also decided I would **NOT prepare 2 meals**. No longer would I be cooking "diet" food for me and "regular" food for the rest of my family. Whatever I cooked, everyone else would be eating too. Therefore, I better prepare food they would eat. *This time, it wasn't going to be a diet. It was to be a permanent lifestyle change.*

Thus I began my "quest" for **good tasting, easy to fix, "normal" food, low in fats, processed sugars and reasonably low in sodium.** I enjoyed experimenting and my kitchen became my science lab. Some of the recipes were new creations; others family favorites I revised, along with requests to update the favorites of friends. But all had to meet the requirements of my new lifestyle or I didn't prepare it.

The word **moderation** best describes **my use of fats, sugar substitutes** and **sodium** in these recipes. Wherever possible, I've used cooking spray for sauteing and browning meats and vegetables. I also use reduced calorie margarine and no fat mayonnaise and salad dressings. Lean ground turkey or ground beef can be used in the recipes. Just be sure either is at least 90% lean.

18

I've also included **small amounts of sugar and brown sugar substitutes as the sweetening agent** in many of the recipes. I don't drink 100 cans of soda a day or eat enough artificially sweetened foods in a 24 hour time period to be troubled by sugar substitutes. But, if this is a concern of yours and you do not need to watch your sugar intake, you can always replace the sugar substitutes with processed sugar.

A word of caution in regards to cooking with **sugar substitutes**. Use **saccharin** based sweeteners when **heating or baking**. In recipes that **don't require heat** Aspartame works well, but leaves an aftertaste in baked products.

I use **eggs** in moderation. I enjoy the real thing on an average of three to four times a week. So, my recipes are calculated on using whole eggs. However, if you choose to use egg substitute in place of the egg, the finished product will turn out just fine and the fat grams per serving will be even lower than those listed.

Whenever **cooked rice or pasta** is an ingredient, follow the package directions, but eliminate the salt and/or margarine called for. This helps lower the sodium and fat content. It tastes just fine, trust me on this.

Most of the recipes are for **4 to 6 servings.** If you don't have this many to feed, you can do what I do; freeze individual portions. Then, all you have to do is choose something from the freezer and take it to work for lunch or have your evening meals prepared in advance for the week. In this way, I always have something on hand both good to eat and good for me.

Unless the recipe includes hard cooked eggs, cream cheese, mayonnaise, or a raw vegetable, **the leftovers will freeze well**. This includes most of the cream pies. Try this on individual servings for your own "TV" dinners.

19

To make life even easier, **whenever a recipe calls for ounce measurements** (other than raw meats) I've included the closest cup equivalent. I need to use my scale daily when creating recipes, so why not measure for you at the same time.

I'm often asked why I use an **8x8 baking dish** in my recipes. It's for portion control. If the recipe says it serves four, just cut down the center, turn the dish and cut again. Like magic, there's your serving. Also, if this is the only recipe you are preparing requiring an oven, the square dish fits into a table top toaster oven easily and energy can be conserved.

You may notice, almost always when I have you open a can of something, such as tomato sauce or evaporated skim milk, I formulate the recipe around the **whole can.** I do this on purpose because I know many of you are like me, not perfect housekeepers and would put the unused portion away with good intentions to use up within a day or two. But, *if and when* you get around to cleaning out the refrigerator, it's still sitting there!

Rarely, if ever, do I have **salt** as an added ingredient. So, I don't tell you to use sodium free products such as tomato sauce. But, if you have a true sodium sensitive condition, I'm trusting you to have "enough smarts" of your own to use the sodium free products, and realize recipes using high sodium ingredients, such as sauerkraut, are to be an occasional treat. I use spices and other flavor enhancing ingredients in such a way, you won't even notice the absence of salt.

Another trick I often use is to include **tiny amounts of "real people" food,** such as coconut, but extend the flavor by using extracts. Try it, you will be surprised by how little of the real thing you can use and still feel you are not being deprived.

Whenever I include **cooked chicken** in a recipe, I use roasted white meat without skin. Whenever, I include **roast beef or pork** in a recipe, I use the loin cuts because they are much leaner. However, most of the time, I do my roasting of all these meats at the local Deli. I just ask for a chunk of their lean roasted meat, such as 6 oz or 8 oz and ask them not to slice it. When I get home, I then cube or dice the meat and am ready to use in my recipe. The reason I do this is three fold. (1) I'm getting just the amount I need without leftovers (2) I don't have the expense of heating the oven (3) I'm not throwing away the bone, gristle and fat I'd be cutting away from the meat. Over all it is probably cheaper to "roast" it the way I do.

I use **canned broth** in place of bouillon to lower the sodium content. The intended flavor is still present in the prepared dish.

After preparing many of my pies and puddings, you may notice I use **nonfat dry milk powder and water** in lots of the recipes. Usually I call for 2/3 cup nonfat dry milk powder and 1 1/4 to 1 1/2 cups water or liquid. I do this on purpose. I can get the nutrients of two cups of milk, but much less liquid. So, the end result is much creamier. Also, the recipe sets up quicker, usually in 5 minutes or less. So if someone is unexpectedly knocking at your door at mealtime, you can quickly throw a pie together and enjoy it minutes later.

Don't give **nonfat dry milk powder** a *"bum steer"*. It's great! I DO NOT use it for drinking, but I DO use it for cooking. Three reasons why are: **(1)** It is very **inexpensive**,(2) It does not **sour** because you use it only as needed 3) you can easily add extra calcium to just about any recipe without added liquid. *Nonfat Dry Milk Powder, Mother Nature's modern day convenience.*

21

Low-fat cooking spray is one of the new wonders to the modern world. It's currently available in three flavors...

Use...**OLIVE** when cooking Mexican or Italian,
...**BUTTER** when the hint of butter is desired and
...**REGULAR** for everything else.

- A quick spray of butter-flavored makes air-popped popcorn a low-fat taste treat.
- It's a good butter substitute on fresh cooked corn on the cob.
- A light spray of the skillet when browning meat makes one think they've used 'old fashioned fat'.
- A quick coating of the casserole before adding the ingredients will make the finished product serve easier and also makes for a quicker clean-up.

If you place 1 cup of **plain fat free yogurt** in a sieve lined with a coffee filter, and place the sieve over a small bowl and refrigerate for about 6 hours, you will end up with a very **good alternative for sour cream.**

To **stabilize yogurt** when cooking or baking with it, just add 1 teaspoon cornstarch to every 3/4 cup yogurt.

If a recipe calls for **evaporated skim milk** and you don't have any in the cupboard, make your own. For every 1/2 cup evaporated skim milk needed, combine 1/3 cup nonfat dry milk powder and 1/2 cup water. Use as you would evaporated skim milk.

A very good **white sauce** for vegetables and casseroles without using added fat can be made by spraying a medium saucepan with butter flavored cooking spray. Place 1 1/2 cups evaporated skim milk and 3 Tablespoons flour in a covered jar. Mix well. Pour into sprayed saucepan and cook over medium heat until thick, stirring constantly. Add salt and pepper to taste. You can also add 1/2 cup canned drained mushrooms and/or 3 oz shredded reduced fat cheese (3/4 cup). Continue cooking until cheese melts.

Heat 2 cups drained **canned or frozen green beans**. Add 1/2 cup **chunky salsa** and heat through. Chunky salsa also makes a wonderful dressing on lettuce salads. It only counts as a vegetable, so enjoy.

The next time you warm **canned vegetables**, such as carrots or green beans, drain and heat the vegetables in **1/4 cup beef or chicken broth.** It gives a nice variation to an old standby.

For **gravy** with all the "old time" flavor but without the extra fat, here is an almost effortless way to prepare it. It's almost as easy as opening up a store bought jar. Pour the juice off the roasted meat. Either place in a large flat bowl and put in the freezer until the fat congeals on top and skim off, or buy one of the new pitchers just made for skimming fat from liquid at your kitchen gadget store. Pour about 2 cups skimmed broth into a medium saucepan. Cook over medium heat. In a covered jar, combine 1/2 cup water or cooled potato broth with 3 tablespoons flour. Mix well. Pour flour mixture into warmed broth. Combine well using a wire whisk. Continue cooking until gravy thickens. Season with salt and pepper to taste.

For a **different taste when preparing sugar free instant pudding** mixes, use 3/4 cup plain fat free yogurt for one of the required cups of milk. Blend as usual. It will be **thicker and creamier.** And, no it doesn't taste like yogurt.

For a special treat that tastes anything but "diet", try placing **spreadable fruit** in a container and microwave for about 15 seconds. Then pour the melted fruit spread over a serving of nonfat ice cream or frozen yogurt. 1 tablespoon of spreadable fruit is equal to 1 fruit serving. Some combinations to get you started are apricot over chocolate ice cream; strawberry over strawberry ice cream, or any flavor over vanilla.

The next time you are making treats for the family, try using **unsweetened applesauce** for some or all of the required oil in the recipe. For instance, if the recipe calls for 1/2 cup cooking oil, use up to the 1/2 cup in applesauce. It works and most people will not even notice the difference. It's great in purchased cake mixes, but so far I haven't been able to figure out a way to deep fat fry with it!

Here's a way to extend the flavor (and oils) of **purchased whipped topping.** Blend together 3/4 cup plain nonfat yogurt and 1/3 cup nonfat dry milk powder. Add sugar substitute to equal 2 Tablespoons sugar, 1 cup Cool Whip Lite and 1 teaspoon of the flavoring of your choice (vanilla, coconut or almond are all good choices). Gently mix and use as you would whipped topping. The texture is almost a cross between marshmallow cream and whipped cream. This is enough to mound high on a pie.

I'm going to let you in on my secret for making **"Grandma's Lemonade".** Use purchased sugar free lemonade mix. Prepare it according to the package directions. Then, slice 1/3 to 1/2 of a lemon, (rind, seeds and all). Pour about 2 cups of the prepared lemonade into a blender. Add the lemon chunks and blend on high for 20-30 seconds or until the lemon almost disappears. Pour back into the pitcher of prepared lemonade and stir well. Serve over ice and enjoy. It tastes just like Grandma used to make...and, I won't tell our secret, if you don't.

The next time you want to enjoy a **"fruit shake" with some pizazz**, just combine soda water and unsweetened fruit juice in a blender. Add crushed ice. Blend on high until thick. Refreshment without guilt.

Another **variation for the sugar free instant vanilla pudding** is to use 1 cup skim milk and 1 cup crushed pineapple juice. Mix as usual.

24

If you are preparing a pie filling that has ample moisture, just line **graham crackers** in the bottom of a 9x9 cake pan. Pour the filling over the top of the crackers. Cover and chill until the moisture has enough time to work down to the crackers and make them soft. Overnight is best. This eliminates the added **fats and sugars of a pie crust.**

In addition to my **family**, I also had an **official tasting team of four co-workers**. None of them need to lose weight, but all enjoy good food. If they gave my creation a "green light", it was included in this collection. If they didn't, I went back to the 'lab' and tried again. Sometimes it was again and again. Some recipes fell into place the first time I experimented with them. But with others I had to revise several times before they were acceptable to my tasters.

I am **not** a Nutritionist, Home Economist or Traditional Food Professional. But, I am probably like most of you, a 'common Jo" who enjoys normal everyday food. What I tried to do with this collection of recipes is bring back the flavor of everyday foods, but prepared in quick yet tasty low fat, low sugar and reasonably low sodium ways.

Healthy Lean Bon Appétit!

Jo Anna

25

A PEEK INTO MY PANTRY AND MY FAVORITE BRANDS

I've been asked many times "What types of foods do you keep on hand and what brands do you use?" There are lots of good products on the grocery shelves today. Many more than we even dreamed about one year ago. And, I can't wait to see what's out there in twelve months. So, the following are my staples and where appropriate, my favorites at this time. I feel these products deliver the most flavor for the least amount of fat, sugar or calories. You may find others you like as well or better. This is only a guide to make your grocery shopping and cooking easier.

Fat Free Plain Yogurt - *Yoplait*
Nonfat Dry Skim Milk Powder - *Carnation*
Evaporated Skim Milk - *Carnation*
Skim Milk
Fat Free Cream Cheese - *Philadelphia*
Fat Free Mayonnaise - *Kraft - 8 calories per Tablespoon*
Fat Free Salad Dressings - *Kraft*
Fat Free Sour Cream - *Land O Lakes*
Reduced Calorie Margarine
    Weight Watcher's, Smart Beat or Promise
Cooking Spray
    Butter - Weight Watcher's
    Olive and Regular - Pam
Cooking Oil - *Puritan Canola Oil*
Sugar Substitute - *White - Sprinkle Sweet or Sugar Twin*
    Brown - Brown Sugar Twin
Reduced Calorie Whipped Topping
    - Cool Whip Lite or La Creme Lite
Sugar Free Gelatin and Pudding Mixes - *Jello*
Baking Mix - *Bisquick Reduced Fat*
Pancake Mix - *Aunt Jemima Lite*
Reduced Calorie Syrup - *Cary's Reduced Calorie Maple*

Reduced Fat Cheese
  - *Kraft, Healthy Choice and Weight Watcher's*
Tomato Sauce - *Hunt's - regular and with tomato bits*
Shredded Frozen Potatoes - *Mr. Dell's*
Spreadable Fruit - *Smucker's, Welch's or Sorrell Ridge*
Peanut Butter - *Jif*
Chicken Broth - *Campbell's Healthy Request*
Beef Broth - *Swanson*
Bacon Bits - *Hormel*
Cream of Mushroom, Chicken or Tomato Soup
  - *Campbell's Healthy Request*
Purchased Pie Crust - *unbaked - Pillsbury - in dairy case*
  Graham, butter flavored or chocolate - Keebler
90% or more lean Pastrami or Corned Beef - *Carl Buddig*
97% Lean Reduced Sodium Ham - *Dubuque*
Lean Frankfurters & Polish Kielbasa Sausage
  - *Healthy Choice*
Canned White Chicken, packed in water - *Swanson*
90% Lean Ground Turkey OR Beef
Canned Tuna, packed in water
Unsweetened Apple Juice
Unsweetened Apple Sauce
Reduced Calorie Bread - 40 calories per slice or less
Hamburger Buns - *Colonial Old Fashion* - 80 calories each
Rice - instant, regular and brown
Noodles, Spaghetti and Macaroni
Frozen Fruit - no sugar added
Fresh Fruit
Salsa
Fresh, Frozen and Canned Vegetables
Spices
Lemon and Lime Juice
Instant Lemonade - *Crystal Light*

If your grocer does not stock these items, why not ask if they can try them on a trial basis. Then if the store responds, be sure to tell your friends so the sales are enough to warrant the shelf space.

The items on my shopping list are normal everyday foods, but are all as low fat and low sugar, (*while still tasting good*), as I can find. I can make any recipe in this cookbook as long as these staples are on my shelves. After using the products for a couple of weeks, you will find it becomes routine to have them on hand. And, I guarantee I DON'T spend any more now at the store than I did two years ago when I told myself I couldn't afford some of these items. But, back then, the unhealthy high priced snacks I really DIDN'T need, somehow made the magic leap from the grocery shelves into my cart. Who was I kidding?

SOUPS

SOUPS

BASIC VEGETABLE SOUP

4 cups canned tomatoes with juice
3 1/2 cups canned beef broth
4 cups coarsely chopped cabbage
2 cups chopped celery
2 cups chopped carrots
1 cup chopped onion
2 Tablespoons lemon juice
1 Tablespoon Sprinkle Sweet

Blend tomatoes in blender on chop for 10 seconds. In large saucepan combine blended tomatoes and beef broth. Add cabbage, celery, carrots, onion, lemon juice and Sprinkle Sweet. Lower heat. Cover and simmer 2 hours.

Serves 8 (1 1/2 cups)
Each serving equals:
HE: 3 1/4 Ve, 10 OC
61 Calories, 1 gm Fa, 3 gm Pr, 11 gm Ca, 613 mg So
Diabetic: 2 Ve

HINT: Lemon juice helps to reduce the effects of the
        vegetables.

CHEESE—VEGETABLE CHOWDER

2 cups Campbell's Healthy Request chicken broth
1 cup sliced carrots
1/2 cup chopped celery
1/2 cup chopped onion
2 cups skim milk
3 Tablespoons flour
3 3/4 oz shredded reduced fat American or
    Cheddar cheese (scant 1 cup)
1 teaspoon parsley flakes
1/8 teaspoon pepper

In medium saucepan combine broth, carrots, celery and onion. Bring mixture to a boil. Reduce heat and simmer until vegetables are tender. In covered jar combine milk and flour. Pour into broth mixture. Add cheese, parsley flakes and pepper. Continue cooking until thick and bubbly, stirring often.

Serves 4 (1 1/2 cups)
Each serving equals:
HE: 1 1/4 Pr, 1 Ve, 1/2 SM, 1/4 Br, 8 OC
160 Calories, 4 gm Fa, 14 gm Pr, 17 gm Ca, 528 mg So
Diabetic: 2 Ve, 1 Mt, 1/2 SM

CHICKEN CORN CHOWDER

4 cups Campbell's Healthy Request chicken broth
2 cups frozen whole kernel corn
5 oz diced cooked chicken breast (1 cup)
1/2 cup canned sliced mushrooms, drained
1 Tablespoon dried onion flakes
1 teaspoon dried parsley flakes
1/8 teaspoon pepper
1 1/2 cups evaporated skim milk
3 Tablespoons flour

In medium saucepan combine broth, corn, chicken, mushrooms, onion flakes, parsley flakes and pepper. Bring mixture to a boil. Reduce heat and simmer about 15 minutes. In covered jar combine evaporated skim milk and flour. Pour into hot soup mixture. Stir well. Lower heat and simmer 10 minutes, stirring often.

Serves 4 (1 1/2 cups)
Each serving equals:
HE:1 1/4 Br, 1 1/4 Pr, 3/4 SM, 1/4 Ve, 8 OC
236 Calories, 2 gm Fa, 23 gm Pr, 32 gm Ca, 466 mg So
Diabetic: 1 1/2 St, 1 Mt, 1 SM

TOMATO SOUP WITH CHEESE DUMPLINGS

6 cups canned tomatoes with juice

1 cup chopped onion

2 teaspoons reduced calorie margarine

1 3/4 cups canned beef broth

1/8 teaspoon lemon pepper

3/4 cup Bisquick reduced fat baking mix

3 oz shredded reduced fat Cheddar cheese (3/4 cup)

1 Tablespoon fresh parsley, chopped
   or 1/2 teaspoon dried flakes

1 egg, beaten or equivalent in egg substitute

Place tomatoes with juice into blender. Process on chop for 10 seconds. In large saucepan saute onion in melted margarine. Add chopped tomatoes with juice, broth and lemon pepper. Stir well. Lower heat and simmer. Meanwhile combine baking mix, cheese and parsley. Add beaten egg. Mix gently to combine. Drop by tablespoon into hot soup. (Should make 8 dumplings). Cover and simmer until dumplings are done, about 10 minutes.

Serves 4 (2 cups)
Each serving equals:
HE: 3 1/2 Ve, 1 1/4 Pr (1/4 limited), 1 Br, 1/4 Fa, 9 OC
263 Calories, 8 gm Fa, 14 gm Pr, 35 gm Ca 1399 mg So
Diabetic: 3 Ve, 1 Mt, 1 St

HINT: If you like your tomatoes sweeter; add 2 teaspoons Sprinkle Sweet and stir just before dropping dumplings into soup.

CREAM OF TOMATO AND RICE SOUP

2 cups canned tomatoes with juice
1 cup canned beef broth
2/3 cup nonfat dry milk powder
1 cup cooked rice
1/2 teaspoon salt
1/8 teaspoon pepper

Blend tomatoes in blender on chop for 10 seconds. Heat broth in medium sauce pan. Add tomatoes, dry milk powder, rice, salt and pepper. Heat and serve.

Serves 2 (1 1/2 cups)
Each serving equals:.
HE: 2 Ve, 1 SM, 1 Br, 10 OC
202 Calories, 1 gm Fa, 12 gm Pr, 36 gm Ca, 1477 mg So
Diabetic: 1 Ve, 1 SM, 1 St

TOMATO — MUSHROOM SOUP

2 teaspoons reduced calorie margarine
1/2 cup chopped onion
1/2 teaspoon dried minced garlic or
   1 clove garlic, minced
2 cups sliced fresh mushrooms
2 cups Campbell's Healthy Request chicken broth
1 3/4 cups Hunt's Chunky Tomato Sauce
1/4 teaspoon lemon pepper
3/4 oz grated Parmesan cheese (1/4 cup)
2 teaspoons dried parsley flakes

In medium saucepan melt margarine. Add onion and garlic. Saute until onion is tender. Add mushrooms, continue to saute 2-3 minutes. Stir in chicken broth, tomato sauce and lemon pepper. Cover. Lower heat and simmer 20 minutes. Pour into soup bowls. Sprinkle each serving with 1 Tablespoon Parmesan cheese and 1/2 teaspoon parsley flakes.

Serves 4 (1 1/4 cups)
Each serving equals:
HE: 3 Ve, 1/4 Fa, 1/4 Pr, 8 OC
108 Calories, 4 gm Fa, 6 gm Pr, 12 gm Ca, 948 mg So
Diabetic: 2 Ve, 1 Free Ve, 1/2 Mt

FRENCH CABBAGE SOUP

4 cups canned mixed vegetable juice
1 3/4 cups canned beef broth
1 pkg dry onion soup mix
1 cup sliced celery
3 cups shredded cabbage
1 cup diced onion

In large saucepan combine vegetable juice, beef broth and dry onion soup mix. Add celery, cabbage and onion. Lower heat, cover and simmer 1 hour.

Serves 6 (1 1/2 cups)
Each serving equals:
HE: 3 Ve, 26 OC
64 Calories, less than 1 gm Fa, 2 gm Pr, 13 gm Ca, 969 mg So
Diabetic: 2 Ve, 1 Free Ve

SWISS POTATO SOUP

1 can Campbell's Healthy Request
   Cream of Mushroom soup
2 cups skim milk
8 oz diced cooked potatoes (1 1/2 cups)
1/8 teaspoon pepper
1/4 teaspoon dry mustard
3 3/4 oz shredded reduced fat Swiss cheese
   (scant 1 cup)
2 teaspoons chopped parsley

In medium saucepan combine soup, milk, potatoes, pepper and dry mustard. Cook over medium heat until potatoes are warmed through. Add cheese and parsley. Continue cooking until cheese melts, stirring often.

Serves 4 (1 1/4 cups)
Each serving equals:
HE: 1 1/4 Pr, 1/2 Br, 1/2 SM, 1/2 Sl, 1 OC
218 Calories, 8 gm Fa, 11 gm Pr, 25 gm Ca, 794 mg So
Diabetic: 1 1/2 St, 1 Mt, 1/2 SM

SPANISH CORN SOUP

2 cups Campbell's Healthy Request chicken broth
1/2 cup chopped onion
4 oz diced cooked chicken breast (scant 1 cup)
2 cups canned tomatoes with juice, chopped
2 cups frozen whole kernel corn
1/2 teaspoon minced garlic
1 teaspoon chili seasoning mix
1/8 teaspoon pepper

In large saucepan combine chicken broth and onion. Cook over low heat until onion is tender. Add chicken, tomatoes, corn, garlic, chili seasoning and pepper. Lower heat. Cover and simmer 20 minutes.

Serves 4   (1 1/2 cups)
Each serving equals:
HE: 1 1/4 Ve, 1 Pr, 1 Br, 8 OC
161 Calories, 2 gm Fa, 14 gm Pr, 22 gm Ca, 464 mg So
Diabetic: 1 Ve, 1 Mt, 1 St

FRANKFURTER RICE SOUP

8 oz diced Healthy Choice 97% fat free frankfurters
1/2 cup chopped onion
1 3/4 cups Hunt's Chunky Tomato Sauce
1 3/4 cups canned beef broth
1 cup cooked rice
1 teaspoon Italian seasoning
1/4 teaspoon lemon pepper
1 Tablespoon Brown Sugar Twin

In large saucepan sprayed with butter flavored cooking spray saute frankfurters and onion until browned. Add tomato sauce, beef broth, rice, Italian seasoning, pepper and Brown Sugar Twin. Lower heat. Cover and simmer 15 minutes.

Serves 4 (1 1/2 cups)
Each serving equals:
HE: 2 Ve, 1 1/3 Pr, 1/2 Br, 10 OC
150 Calories 3 gm Fa, 10 gm Pr, 21 gm Ca, 1557 mg So
Diabetic: 1 Mt, 1 Ve, 1 St

SALADS

R. VanStel
8/91

SALADS

CUCUMBER TOMATO SALAD

2 cups sliced cucumbers
1 1/2 cups chopped fresh tomatoes
1/4 cup chopped green bell pepper
1/4 cup sliced red onion
1/4 cup wine vinegar
1/4 cup white vinegar
1 Tablespoon fat free Italian dressing
   (4 calories per Tablespoon)
Sugar substitute to equal 2 Tablespoons sugar

In large bowl combine cucumbers, tomatoes, green pepper and onion. In small bowl combine vinegars, Italian dressing and sugar substitute. Pour over vegetables. Cover and chill at least 2 hours.

Serves 4 (3/4 cup)
Each serving equals:
HE: 2 Ve, 4 OC
30 calories, 0 gm Fa, 1 gm Pr, 7gm Ca, 42 mg So
Diabetic: 1 Ve

CREAMY CUCUMBERS

4 cups sliced cucumbers
1/2 cup sliced onion
1/2 cup fat free Ranch dressing
    (20 calories per Tablespoon)
1/4 teaspoon salt
1/8 teaspoon pepper

In large bowl combine cucumbers and onions. Pour dressing over cucumbers and onions. Add salt and pepper. Stir gently to combine. Cover. Chill at least 2 hours.

Serves 4 (1 full cup)
Each serving equals:
HE: 2 1/4 Ve, 1/2 Sl
57 Calories, 0 gm Fa, 1 gm Pr, 13 gm Ca, 436 mg So
Diabetic: 2 Ve

TOMATOES "N" CREAM

2 cups coarsely chopped fresh tomatoes
1/2 cup chopped Bermuda onion
1/4 cup fat free Ranch dressing
    (20 calories per Tablespoon)

In medium bowl combine tomatoes and onion. Pour Ranch dressing over tomato mixture. Stir gently to combine. Cover and chill at least 2 hours.

Serves 4 (3/4 cup)
Each serving equals:
HE: 1 1/4 Ve, 20 OC
45 calories, 0 gm Fa, 1 gm Pr, 10 gm Ca, 159 mg So
Diabetic: 2 Ve

TOMATO SLICES IN BASIL VINAIGRETTE

2 cups fresh sliced tomatoes
1/3 cup white vinegar
1 Tablespoon vegetable oil
1 Tablespoon finely chopped fresh basil
    or 1 teaspoon dried basil
Sugar substitute to equal 1 teaspoon sugar
1/2 teaspoon salt
1/8 teaspoon pepper

Place tomatoes in a shallow dish. In covered jar combine vinegar, oil, basil, sugar substitute, salt and pepper. Shake well. Pour mixture over tomatoes. Cover and chill at least 2 hours.

Serves 4 (1/2 cup)
Each serving equals:
HE: 1 Ve, 3/4 Fa
46 calories, 3 gm Fa, 1 gm Pr, 4 gm Ca, 272 mg So
Diabetic: 1 Ve, 1/2 Fa

DEVILED LETTUCE

6 cups shredded lettuce
1/2 cup chopped celery
1/4 cup chopped green bell pepper
1/4 cup chopped onion
1 (8 oz) pkg fat free cream cheese
1/2 cup fat free mayonnaise
    (8 calories per Tablespoon)
6 oz finely diced Dubuque 97% fat free ham (1 full cup)
1 Tablespoon prepared mustard
1 Tablespoon Brown Sugar Twin

In large bowl combine lettuce, celery, green pepper and onion. Layer on bottom of large low sided serving bowl. In medium bowl stir cream cheese with spoon until soft. Add mayonnaise, ham, mustard and Brown Sugar Twin. Drop cream cheese mixture by spoonfuls on top of lettuce. Cover and chill. Toss just before serving .

Serves 8 (1 cup)
Each serving equals:
HE: 1 3/4 Ve, 1 Pr, 8 OC
67 calories, 1 gm Fa, 8 gm Pr, 6 gm Ca, 511 mg So
Diabetic: 1 Ve, 1 Mt

CARROT SALAD

2 3/4 cups grated carrots
1/2 cup chopped celery
1/4 cup chopped green bell pepper
1/4 cup fat free mayonnaise
   (8 calories per Tablespoon)
1 Tablespoon white vinegar
Sugar substitute to equal 2 teaspoons sugar
1 teaspoon prepared horseradish

In medium bowl combine carrots, celery and green pepper. In small bowl combine mayonnaise, vinegar, sugar substitute and horseradish. Pour over carrot mixture. Mix well to combine. Cover and chill.

Serves 4 (3/4 cup)
Each serving equals:
HE: 1 3/4 Ve, 9 OC
48 calories, 0 gm Fa, 1 gm Pr, 11 gm Ca, 166 mg So
Diabetic: 2 Ve

GARDEN SALAD

3 cups cooked rotini noodles
1 cup chopped carrots
1 cup chopped celery
1 cup frozen peas, thawed
1/2 cup diced green bell pepper
1/2 cup chopped onion
1 cup chopped broccoli
1/8 teaspoon lemon pepper
1 cup fat free French dressing
    (20 calories per Tablespoon)

In large bowl combine noodles, carrots, celery, peas, green pepper, onion and broccoli. Add lemon pepper and French dressing. Mix well to combine. Cover and chill several hours.

Serves 8 (1 cup)
Each serving equals:
HE: 1 Br, 1 Ve, 1/2 Sl
139 calories, less than 1 gm Fa, 4 gm Pr, 29 gm Ca, 282 mg So
Diabetic: 2 Ve, 1 St

GREEN BEAN—CARROT SALAD

2 cups canned green beans, drained
2 cups canned sliced carrots, drained
1/4 cup thinly sliced onion
1/4 cup chopped green bell pepper
1/2 cup chopped celery
2 Tablespoons snipped fresh parsley
1/3 cup white vinegar
Sugar substitute to equal 4 teaspoons sugar
4 teaspoons vegetable oil
1/2 teaspoon dry mustard
1/4 teaspoon lemon pepper

In medium bowl combine green beans, carrots, onion, green pepper, celery and parsley. In covered jar combine vinegar, sugar substitute, oil, mustard, and lemon pepper. Shake well. Pour mixture over vegetables. Stir to coat. Cover and chill several hours.

Serves 8 (2/3 cup)
Each serving equals:
HE: 1 1/4 Ve, 1/2 Fa , 2 OC
42 calories, 2 gm Fa, 1 gm Pr, 5 gm Ca, 180 mg So
Diabetic: 1 Ve, 1/2 Fa

CABBAGE AND CARROT SALAD

2 cups shredded cabbage
1/2 cup shredded carrots
1 teaspoon vinegar
1/4 cup fat free mayonnaise
    (8 calories per Tablespoon)
Sugar substitute to equal 1 teaspoon sugar
1/4 teaspoon salt
1/8 teaspoon pepper

In large bowl combine vinegar, mayonnaise, sugar substitute, salt and pepper. Add carrots and cabbage. Mix well to combine. Cover and chill at least 1 hour.

Serves 2 (1 cup)
Each serving equals:
HE: 2 1/2 Ve, 17 OC
54 Calories, 0 gm Fa, 1 gm Pr, 13 gm Ca, 539 mg So
Diabetic: 2 Ve

CALICO COLESLAW

4 cups shredded cabbage
1 1/2 cups shredded carrots
1/2 cup diced onions
1 cup frozen peas, thawed
1/4 cup Bacon Bits
1 1/2 oz Parmesan cheese (1/2 cup)
1 cup fat free mayonnaise
   (8 calories per Tablespoon)
Sugar substitute to equal 1 Tablespoon sugar
1/8 teaspoon lemon pepper

In large bowl combine cabbage, carrots, onions, peas, Bacon Bits and Parmesan cheese. In small bowl combine mayonnaise, sugar substitute and lemon pepper. Pour mayonnaise mixture over cabbage. Mix well. Chill several hours.

Serves 8 (3/4 cup)
Each serving equals:
HE: 1 1/2 Ve, 1/4 Br, 1/4 Pr, 32 OC
161 Calories, 6 gm Fa, 11 gm Pr, 16 gm Ca, 701 mg So
Diabetic: 2 Ve, 1 Free Ve, 1 Fa, 1/2 Mt

PINEAPPLE COLE SLAW

2 cups shredded cabbage
1/4 cup chopped green bell pepper
1/4 cup chopped celery
1 Tablespoon dried onion flakes
1 cup canned pineapple chunks,
    packed in its own juice (drained)
1/4 cup white vinegar
Sugar substitute to equal 1 Tablespoon sugar

In medium bowl combine cabbage, green pepper, celery, onion flakes and pineapple chunks. In small bowl combine vinegar and sugar substitute. Add to cabbage mixture. Toss well to combine. Cover. Chill at least 2 hours before serving.

Serves 2 (1 cup)
Each serving equals:
HE: 2 1/2 Ve, 1 Fr, 3 OC
118 Calories, 0 gm Fa, 2 gm Pr, 28 gm Ca, 16 mg So
Diabetic: 2 Ve, 1 Fr

WALDORF COLESLAW

4 cups shredded cabbage
2 small apples, cored and chopped (1 cup)
1/2 cup raisins
2 oz chopped peanuts (1/2 cup)
3/4 cup plain fat free yogurt
1/3 cup nonfat dry milk powder
1/2 cup fat free mayonnaise
    (8 calories per Tablespoon)
Sugar substitute to equal 1 Tablespoon sugar

In large bowl combine cabbage, apples, raisins and peanuts. In small bowl combine yogurt and dry milk powder. Add mayonnaise and sugar substitute. Mix well. Blend into cabbage. Toss lightly. Chill several hours before serving.

Serves 8 (3/4 cup)
Each serving equals:
HE: 1 Ve, 3/4 Fr, 1/2 Fa, 1/4 Pr, 1/4 SM, 9 OC
133 Calories, 4 gm Fa, 5 gm Pr, 20 gm Ca, 165 mg So
Diabetic: 1 Fr, 1 Ve, 1 Fa

ZESTY COLESLAW

3 cups shredded cabbage
1 cup shredded carrots
1/4 cup chopped green bell pepper
1/4 cup chopped red onion
1/4 cup cider vinegar
 2 Tablespoons Brown Sugar Twin
1 Tablespoon vegetable oil
1/2 teaspoon dry mustard
1/2 teaspoon salt

In a large bowl combine cabbage, carrots, green pepper and onion. In a covered jar combine vinegar, Brown Sugar Twin, vegetable oil, dry mustard and salt. Shake well. Pour over cabbage mixture. Toss well to coat vegetables. Cover and chill at least 4 hours.

Serves 6 (3/4 cup)
Each serving equals:
HE: 1 1/2 Ve, 1/2 Fa, 2 OC
43 Calories, 2 gm Fa, 1 gm Pr, 6 gm Ca, 15 mg So
Diabetic: 1 Ve, 1/2 Fa

MEXICAN CORN SALAD

2 cups canned whole kernel corn, drained
1/4 cup chopped onion
1/4 cup chopped green bell pepper
1 oz sliced pimento stuffed green olives(1/4 cup)
1/4 cup fat free mayonnaise
    (8 calories per Tablespoon)
1 teaspoon chili seasoning mix
1/4 teaspoon salt
1/8 teaspoon pepper

In a medium bowl combine corn, onion, green pepper and olives. In small bowl combine mayonnaise, chili seasoning mix, salt and pepper. Blend into corn mixture. Cover and chill at least 2 hours.

Serves 4 (2/3 cup)
Each serving equals:
HE: 1 Br, 1/4 Ve, 1/4 Fa, 8 OC
91 Calories, 1 gm Fa, 2 gm Pr, 19 gm Ca, 669 mg So
Diabetic: 1 St

KIDNEY BEAN SALAD

20 oz canned red kidney beans, rinsed and drained
2 hard boiled eggs, chopped
1 cup chopped celery
1/2 cup fat free Ranch dressing
    (18 calories per Tablespoon)
1/8 teaspoon pepper

In large bowl combine kidney beans, chopped eggs and celery. Add Ranch dressing and pepper. Mix well to combine. Cover and chill.

Serves 8 (1/2 cup)
Each serving equals:
HE: 1 1/2 Pr (1/4 limited), 1/4 Ve, 18 OC
112 Calories, 2 gm Fa, 6 gm Pr, 18 gm Ca, 468 mg So
Diabetic: 1 Mt, 1 St

HINT: 1) A 16 oz can of kidney beans is usually 10 oz drained weight.
　　　2) To lower the fat grams even more, toss the egg yolk in the trash can and chop only the egg white.

BLUEBERRY SALAD

2 (4 serving) pkgs sugar free raspberry gelatin
2 cups boiling water
1 cup canned crushed pineapple,
     packed in its own juice, drained (reserve liquid)
2 teaspoons lemon juice
3 cups fresh blueberries or frozen, thawed and drained
1 cup chopped celery

In large bowl combine dry gelatin and boiling water. Mix well to dissolve gelatin. Add enough water to reserved pineapple juice to make 1 cup liquid; add lemon juice to liquid. Blend liquid into gelatin mixture. Cool slightly. Stir in blueberries, pineapple and celery. Pour into 8 x 8 dish. Chill until set.

Serves 8
Each serving equals:
HE: 3/4 Fr, 1/4 Ve, 8 OC
63 Calories, 0 gm Fa, 2 gm Pr, 14 gm Ca, 71 mg So
Diabetic: 1 Fr

LIME PEAR SALAD

1 cup boiling water
2 cups canned pears, packed in its own juice,
    drained and chopped (reserve juice)
1 (4 serving) pkg sugar free lime gelatin
3/4 cup fat free cottage cheese

In medium bowl combine boiling water and reserved pear juice. Add dry gelatin. Mix well to dissolve gelatin. Chill for about 15 minutes. Stir in cottage cheese. Whip with wire whisk until fluffy. Add pears. Mix gently to combine. Pour into 8 x 8 dish. Chill until set.

Serves 6
Each serving equals:
HE: 2/3 Fr, 1/4 Pr, 5 OC
65 Calories, 0 gm Fa, 5 gm Pr, 12 gm Ca, 145 mg So
Diabetic: 1 Fr

RED RASPBERRY SALAD

2 (4 serving) pkgs sugar free raspberry gelatin
2 cups boiling water
2 1/4 cups frozen red raspberries (no sugar added)
1 1/2 cups unsweetened applesauce
3/4 cup plain fat free yogurt
1/3 cup nonfat dry milk powder
Sugar substitute to equal 1 Tablespoon sugar
1/2 cup reduced calorie whipped topping
    (8 calories per Tablespoon)
1/4 teaspoon vanilla extract
2 oz miniature marshmallows (1 cup)

In large bowl combine dry gelatin with boiling water.
Mix well to dissolve gelatin. Cool 5 minutes. Blend in
raspberries and applesauce. Pour into 9 x 13 dish.
Chill until set. In small bowl combine yogurt and dry
milk powder. Blend in sugar substitute, whipped
topping and vanilla extract. Fold in marshmallows.
Spread mixture evenly on top of set gelatin mixture.
Chill until ready to serve.

Serves 8
Each serving equals:
HE: 3/4 Fr, 1/4 SM, 29 OC
97 Calories, less than 1 gm Fa, 4 gm Pr, 19 gm Ca, 91 mg So
Diabetic: 1 Fr, 1/2 St

REFRESHING RHUBARB RELISH

2 cups diced rhubarb
1/2 cup hot water
1 (4 serving) pkg sugar free raspberry,
   strawberry or lemon gelatin
1 cup cold water
2 small apples, cored and chopped (1 cup)
1/4 cup raisins
1 1/2 oz chopped walnuts(1/3 cup)

In medium saucepan cook rhubarb in hot water until soft. Dissolve dry gelatin in hot rhubarb sauce. Add cold water and stir well. Blend in apples, raisins and walnuts. Mix gently to combine. Pour into 8 x 8 dish. Chill until set.

Serves 6
Each serving equals:
HE: 2/3 Fr, 2/3 Ve, 1/2 Fa, 1/4 Pr, 5 OC
94 Calories, 4 gm Fa, 3 gm Pr, 12 gm Ca, 39 mg So
Diabetic: 1 Fr, 1 Fa

HINT: Good served with 1 teaspoon fat free mayonnaise on top. If used, count optional calories accordingly.

STRAWBERRY SALAD

3/4 cup plain fat free yogurt

1/3 cup nonfat dry milk powder

1/2 cup reduced calorie whipped topping
   (8 calories per Tablespoon)

Sugar substitute to equal 1 Tablespoon sugar

4 cups frozen strawberries, thawed and sliced
   (no sugar added)

1 cup canned crushed pineapple,
   packed in its own juice, drained

2 oz miniature marshmallows (1 cup)

In medium bowl combine yogurt and dry milk powder. Blend in whipped topping and sugar substitute. Add strawberries, pineapple and marshmallows. Mix gently to combine. Spoon into 6 dessert dishes. Chill at least 2 hours.

Serves 6
Each serving equals:
HE: 1 Fr, 1/3 SM, 28 OC
126 Calories, 1 gm Fa, 4 gm Pr, 26 gm Ca, 51 mg So
Diabetic: 1 Fr, 1/2 SM

STRAWBERRY RICE SALAD

1 (4 serving) pkg sugar free strawberry gelatin
1/2 cup boiling water
2 cups canned crushed pineapple
   packed in its own juice, undrained
2 cups cooked rice
1 cup reduced calorie whipped topping
   (8 calories per Tablespoon)
3/4 cup plain fat free yogurt
1/2 teaspoon vanilla extract

In medium bowl combine dry gelatin and boiling water. Mix well to dissolve gelatin. Blend in pineapple with juice. Stir in rice. Let partially set (about 1 hour). Stir in whipped topping, yogurt and vanilla extract. Chill until ready to serve.

Serves 4 (1 cup)
Each serving equals:
HE: 1 Br, 1 Fr, 1/4 SM, 1 Sl
207 Calories, 2 gm Fa, 6 gm Pr, 42 gm Ca, 93 mg So
Diabetic: 2 St, 1 Fr

GLORIFIED RICE

2 cups cooked rice
2 cups fruit cocktail, packed in its
    own juice, drained
1 oz miniature marshmallows (1/2 cup)
3/4 cup plain fat free yogurt
1/3 cup nonfat dry milk powder
3/4 cup reduced calorie whipped topping
    (8 calories per Tablespoon)
Sugar substitute to equal 2 Tablespoons sugar
1 teaspoon almond extract

In medium bowl combine rice, fruit cocktail and marshmallows. In small bowl combine yogurt and dry milk powder. Stir in whipped topping, sugar substitute and almond extract. Blend into rice mixture. Chill at least 2 hours.

Serves 4 (1 cup)
Each serving equals:
HE: 1 Br, 1 Fr, 1/2 SM, 1/2 Sl
216 Calories, 2 gm Fa, 6 gm Pr, 44 gm Ca, 78 mg So
Diabetic: 2 St, 1 Fr

HOLIDAY SALAD

BOTTOM
1 (4 serving) pkg sugar free lime gelatin
1 1/2 cups boiling water

MIDDLE
8 oz fat free cream cheese
1 cup canned crushed pineapple, packed in
    its own juice (drained)
Sugar substitute to equal 2 teaspoons sugar
1/2 teaspoon vanilla extract
1 oz chopped pecans (1/4 cup)

TOP
1 (4 serving) pkg sugar free strawberry gelatin
1 1/2 cups boiling water

Prepare bottom layer by mixing dry lime gelatin and 1 1/2 cups boiling water in medium bowl. Pour into an 8x8 dish. Chill until set.

In medium bowl stir cream cheese with spoon until soft. Add pineapple, sugar substitute, vanilla extract and pecans. Spread over set lime layer. Chill about 1 hour.

Prepare top layer by mixing dry strawberry gelatin and 1 1/2 cups boiling water in medium bowl. Pour over cream cheese layer. Chill several hours.

Serves 8
Each serving equals:
HE: 1/2 Pr, 1/2 Fa, 1/4 Fr, 8 OC
72 Calories, 2 gm Fa, 6 gm Pr, 7 gm Ca, 225 mg So
Diabetic: 1/2 Fr, 1/2 Mt

5 - CUP SALAD

1 cup canned mandarin oranges,
    rinsed and drained
1 cup canned pineapple chunks,
    packed in its own juice, drained
2 Tablespoons shredded coconut
1 oz miniature marshmallows (1/2 cup)
3/4 cup plain fat free yogurt
Sugar substitute to equal 4 teaspoons sugar
1 teaspoon coconut extract

In medium bowl combine orange sections, pineapple chunks, coconut and marshmallows. In small bowl combine yogurt, sugar substitute and coconut extract. Add to orange mixture. Mix gently to combine. Cover and chill at least 2 hours.

Serves 4 (2/3 cup)
Each serving equals:
HE: 1 Fr, 1/4 SM, 22 OC
128 Calories, 1 gm Fa, 3 gm Pr, 27 gm Ca, 49 mg So
Diabetic: 2 Fr

LEMON LIME APPLESAUCE SALAD

3 cups unsweetened applesauce
2 (4 serving) pkgs sugar free lemon gelatin
1 cup diet lemon-lime soda
3/4 cup plain fat free yogurt
1/3 cup nonfat dry milk powder
1 cup reduced calorie whipped topping
    (8 calories per Tablespoon)

In medium saucepan heat applesauce to boiling. Remove from heat. Stir in dry gelatin. Mix well to dissolve gelatin. Add lemon-lime soda. Chill 30 minutes. In large bowl combine yogurt and dry milk powder. Stir in whipped topping. Gently fold yogurt mixture into gelatin mixture. Pour into 8 x 8 dish. Chill at least 3 hours.

Serves 8
Each serving equals:
HE: 3/4 Fr, 1/4 SM, 24 OC
78 Calories, 1 gm Fa, 3 gm Pr, 15 gm Ca, 78 mg So
Diabetic: 1 Fr

MANDARIN ORANGE SALAD

1 (4 serving) pkg sugar free orange gelatin
1 cup boiling water
1/2 cup cold water
1 cup canned crushed pineapple, packed in
    its own juice, undrained
1 cup canned mandarin oranges, rinsed and drained
3/4 cup plain fat free yogurt
1/3 cup nonfat dry milk powder
1 cup reduced calorie whipped topping
    (8 calories per Tablespoon)

In large bowl combine dry gelatin and boiling water. Stir in cold water and pineapple with juice. Blend in oranges. Chill 30 minutes. In medium bowl combine yogurt and dry milk powder. Blend in whipped topping. Gently fold yogurt mixture into gelatin mixture. Pour into 8 x 8 dish. Chill at least 3 hours.

Serves 8
Each serving equals:
HE: 1/2 Fr, 1/4 SM, 20 OC
73 Calories, 1 gm Fa, 3 gm Pr, 13 gm Ca, 62 mg So
Diabetic: 1 Fr

DIJON CHICKEN SALAD

2 Tablespoons fat free mayonnaise
   (8 calories per Tablespoon)
2 teaspoons Dijon mustard
1 Tablespoon finely chopped onion
4 oz diced cooked chicken breast (scant 1 cup)
1/8 teaspoon lemon pepper

In medium bowl combine mayonnaise, mustard and onion. Add chicken and lemon pepper. Toss gently to combine. Serve on lettuce as a salad or use as a sandwich filling.

Serves 2 (1/2 cup)
Each serving equals:
HE: 2 Pr, 8 OC
111 Calories, 3 gm Fa, 18 gm Pr, 3 gm Ca, 339 mg So
Diabetic: 2 Mt

ALMOND CHICKEN SALAD

6 oz diced cooked chicken breast (full 1 cup)
1 oz toasted slivered almonds (1/4 cup)
1/2 cup chopped celery
1/3 cup fat free mayonnaise
    (8 calories per Tablespoon)
1 Tablespoon lemon juice
1 Tablespoon chopped fresh parsley or
    1 teaspoon dried parsley
1/4 teaspoon salt
1/8 teaspoon pepper

In medium bowl combine chicken, almonds and celery. In small bowl combine mayonnaise, lemon juice, parsley, salt and pepper. Blend into chicken mixture and toss lightly. Chill until ready to serve.

Serves 4 (1/2 cup)
Each serving equals:
HE: 1 3/4 Pr, 1/2 Fa, 1/4 Ve,11 OC
129 Calories, 5 gm Fa, 15 gm Pr, 6 gm Ca, 403 mg So
Diabetic: 2 Mt

CHICKEN WALDORF SALAD

4 oz diced cooked chicken breast (scant 1 cup)
1 small apple, cored and diced (1/2 cup)
1/2 cup chopped celery
2 Tablespoons raisins
1/4 cup fat free mayonnaise
    (8 calories per Tablespoon)

In small bowl combine chicken, apple, celery and raisins. Blend in mayonnaise. Chill. Serve on lettuce leaf.

Serves 2 (3/4 cup)
Each serving equals:
HE: 2 Pr, 1 Fr, 1/4 Ve, 16 OC
191 Calories, 2 gm Fa, 18 gm Pr, 25 gm Ca, 407 mg So
Diabetic: 2 Mt, 1 Fr, 1/2 St

POLYNESIAN SALAD

1 Tablespoon + 1 teaspoon reduced
   calorie margarine
2 Tablespoons Brown Sugar Twin
6 oz diced Dubuque 97% fat free ham (full 1 cup)
4 cups cooked elbow macaroni
2 cups canned pineapple chunks, packed in its own
   juice (drained), reserving 2 Tablespoons juice
3 oz shredded reduced fat Cheddar or American
   cheese (3/4 cup)
1/2 cup chopped green bell pepper
1/2 cup fat free mayonnaise
   (8 calories per Tablespoon)
3/4 cup plain fat free yogurt
1/3 cup nonfat dry milk powder
1/2 teaspoon salt

In large skillet melt margarine with Brown Sugar Twin;
add diced ham. Cook and stir until ham is golden
brown. Cool. In large bowl combine macaroni,
pineapple, cheese and green pepper. In small bowl
combine mayonnaise, yogurt, dry milk powder,
reserved pineapple juice and salt. Stir into macaroni
mixture. Blend in cooled ham mixture. Chill at least 2
hours.

Serves 8 (1 cup)
Each serving equals:
HE: 1 Br, 1 Pr, 1/2 Fr, 1/4 Fa, 1/4 SM, 10 OC
227 Calories, 3 gm Fa, 12 gm Pr, 37 gm Ca, 609 mg So
Diabetic: 1 1/2 St, 1 Fr, 1 Mt

VEGETABLES

CELERY

R.Pelletier 8/91

VEGETABLES

GREEN BEANS AND STUFFING SUPREME

1 can Campbell's Healthy Request
   Cream of Mushroom soup
1 Tablespoon flour
3/4 cup plain fat free yogurt
1 Tablespoon dried onion flakes
1/4 teaspoon salt
1/8 teaspoon pepper
4 cups frozen green beans, cooked and drained
2 cups Campbell's Healthy Request chicken broth
3 oz herb seasoned stuffing mix (2 cups)

Preheat oven to 350 degrees. In saucepan combine soup, flour, yogurt, onion, salt and pepper. Stir in green beans. Spray an 8x8 baking dish with butter flavored cooking spray. Pour mixture into dish. In medium bowl combine broth and dry stuffing mix. Stir until blended and soft. Evenly sprinkle stuffing mixture on top of bean mixture. Cover. Bake 25 minutes; uncover and bake additional 5 minutes.

Serves 4
Each serving equals:
HE: 2 Ve, 1 Br, 1/4 SM, 1/2 Sl, 17 OC
205 Calories, 3 gm Fa, 9 gm Pr, 36 gm Ca, 741 mg So
Diabetic: 2 Ve, 2 St

HINT: Brownberry bread cubes work great.

GREEN BEAN MELODY

2 cups cooked rotini noodles
3 cups frozen green beans, cooked and drained
1 cup canned sliced mushrooms, drained
1 can Campbell's Healthy Request
   Cream of Mushroom soup
1/2 teaspoon lemon pepper
1/2 teaspoon dried basil
1 Tablespoon + 1 teaspoon reduced calorie margarine
1 1/2 oz grated Parmesan cheese (1/2 cup)

In large saucepan combine noodles and green beans. Stir in mushrooms. Add soup, lemon pepper and basil. Mix well. Add margarine and cheese. Continue cooking until heated through.

Serves 6 (1 cup)
Each serving equals:
HE: 1 1/3 Ve, 2/3 Br, 1/3 Fa, 1/3 Pr, 28 OC
153 Calories, 4 gm Fa, 7 gm Pr, 22 gm Ca, 741 mg So
Diabetic: 1 Ve, 1 St, 1/2 Mt

PERKY GREEN BEANS

3 cups fresh or frozen green beans
1 Tablespoon + 1 teaspoon reduced calorie
   margarine
1 oz slivered almonds (1/4 cup)
2 teaspoons lemon juice
1/8 teaspoon lemon pepper

In medium saucepan cook beans in water until tender. Drain. Transfer beans to serving dish and keep warm. Meanwhile in small skillet melt margarine. Stir in almonds, lemon juice and lemon pepper. Cook over medium heat until heated through. Pour mixture over beans. Toss gently to combine. Serve at once.

Serves 4 (3/4 cup)
Each serving equals:
HE: 1 1/2 Ve, 1 Fa, 1/4 Pr
84 Calories, 5 gm Fa, 3 gm Pr, 7 gm Ca, 23 mg So
Diabetic: 1 1/2 Ve, 1 Fa

BROCCOLI WITH ZEST

1 1/2 cups evaporated skim milk
3 Tablespoons flour
1/4 teaspoon lemon pepper
1 teaspoon prepared mustard
1 teaspoon prepared horseradish
3 cups frozen cut broccoli, cooked and drained

In covered jar combine evaporated skim milk, flour and lemon pepper. Pour into medium saucepan sprayed with butter flavored cooking spray. Cook over medium heat, stirring constantly until mixture thickens. Stir in mustard and horseradish. Add broccoli and stir until blended.

Serves 4 (3/4 cup)
Each serving equals:
HE: 1 1/2 Ve, 3/4 SM, 1/4 Br
116 Calories, 0 gm Fa, 10 gm Pr, 19 gm Ca, 145 mg So
Diabetic: 1 1/2 Ve, 1 SM

HINT: A 16 oz. bag of frozen broccoli is 3 cups.

CABBAGE CARROT CURRY

4 cups coarsely chopped cabbage
1 cup shredded carrots
1/2 teaspoon curry powder
1/4 teaspoon mustard seed
1/8 teaspoon pepper
2/3 cup nonfat dry milk powder
1/2 cup water
1 Tablespoon + 1 teaspoon reduced
   calorie margarine

In large skillet sprayed with butter flavored cooking spray, combine cabbage, carrots, curry powder, mustard seed and pepper. In small bowl combine dry milk powder and water. Add milk mixture and margarine to cabbage mixture. Cover. Cook over medium heat until cabbage is tender and liquid is absorbed, about 6 minutes.

Serves 4 (1 cup)
Each serving equals:
HE: 2 1/2 Ve, 1/2 Fa 1/2 SM
79 Calories, 1 gm Fa, 5 gm Pr, 12 gm Ca, 100 mg So
Diabetic: 1 Ve, 1/2 SM

CARROTS AU GRATIN

4 cups sliced fresh carrots
1/4 cup chopped onion
1/4 cup chopped green bell pepper
2 oz Ritz crackers, crushed (1 cup)
1/8 teaspoon lemon pepper
1 Tablespoon + 1 teaspoon reduced
    calorie margarine, melted
3 oz shredded reduced fat Cheddar cheese (3/4 cup)

Preheat oven to 425 degrees. In large saucepan cook carrots in boiling water until crisp tender. Drain. In skillet sprayed with butter flavored cooking spray saute onion and green pepper until tender. In a large bowl combine crackers, onions, green pepper and lemon pepper. Spray an 8x8 baking dish with butter flavored cooking spray. Alternate 2 layers of carrots and crumb mixture, ending with crumbs. Pour melted margarine over top and sprinkle with cheese. Bake 15-20 minutes or until cheese melts.

Serves 6
Each serving equals:
HE: 1 1/2 Ve, 2/3 Pr, 1/3 Fa, 1/3 Br, 20 OC
125 Calories, 5 gm Fa, 5 gm Pr, 14 gm Ca, 227 mg So
Diabetic: 1 Ve, 1/2 Mt, 1/2 Fa, 1/2 St

CHEDDAR CHEESE CARROT QUICHE

1 cup shredded carrots
1/3 cup nonfat dry milk powder
1/2 cup water
2 eggs or equivalent in egg substitute
2 Tablespoons chopped green onion
1/8 teaspoon lemon pepper
1/4 teaspoon ginger
3 oz shredded reduced fat Cheddar cheese (3/4 cup)

Preheat oven to 350 degrees. In a medium saucepan cook carrots with about 1" of water. Bring to boil. Cover and remove from heat. Let stand 5 minutes; then drain. In medium bowl combine dry milk powder, water, eggs, onion and seasonings until blended. Stir in drained carrots and cheese. Spray 9" pie plate or quiche pan with butter flavored cooking spray. Pour carrot mixture into baking dish. Place dish in pan of hot water. Bake 35 minutes or until knife inserted in center comes out clean.

Serves 4
Each serving equals:
HE: 1 1/2 Pr (1/2 limited),1/2 Ve, 1/4 SM
123 Calories, 5 gm Fa, 12 gm Pr, 7 gm Ca, 243 mg So
Diabetic: 1 1/2 Mt, 1 Ve

AU GRATIN CABBAGE

7 1/2 cups chopped cabbage
1 can Campbell's Healthy Request
    Cream of Mushroom soup
3 3/4 oz shredded reduced fat Cheddar cheese
    (scant 1 cup)
1 Tablespoon flour
1/8 teaspoon pepper
1 1/2 oz dried bread crumbs (6 Tablespoons)
3/4 oz grated Parmesan cheese (1/4 cup)
1 teaspoon dried parsley flakes

Preheat oven to 350 degrees. In large saucepan cook cabbage in boiling water until tender, about 6 minutes. Drain. Combine soup, cheese, flour and pepper in saucepan. Heat, stirring until cheese melts. Combine with cabbage. Spray an 8 x 8 baking dish with butter flavored cooking spray. Place cabbage mixture in casserole. Toss bread crumbs with Parmesan cheese and parsley flakes. Sprinkle on top of cabbage. Quickly spray with butter flavored cooking spray. Bake 15 minutes or until thoroughly heated.

Serves 6
Each serving equals:
HE: 2 1/2 Ve, 1 Pr, 1/3 Br, 33 OC
140 Calories, 5 gm Fa, 9 gm Pr, 15 gm Ca, 491 mg So
Diabetic 2 Ve, 1 Mt, 1/2 St

CORN—ZUCCHINI BAKE

2 cups sliced zucchini
1/2 cup chopped onion
2 eggs, beaten or equivalent in egg substitute
2 cups frozen whole kernel corn, thawed
1 1/2 oz shredded reduced fat Swiss cheese(1/3 cup)
1 1/2 oz shredded reduced fat Cheddar cheese
　　(1/3 cup)
3/4 oz dry bread crumbs (3 Tablespoons)
3/4 oz grated Parmesan cheese (1/4 cup)
1 teaspoon dried parsley flakes

Preheat oven to 350 degrees. In a covered medium saucepan cook zucchini in water until tender, about 15-20 minutes. Drain and mash with fork. In skillet sprayed with butter flavored cooking spray, saute onions until tender. Add mashed zucchini, eggs, corn and cheese. Mix well to combine. Pour into 8x8 baking dish sprayed with butter flavored cooking spray. In small bowl, combine bread crumbs, Parmesan cheese and parsley flakes. Sprinkle on top of zucchini mixture. Quickly spray with butter flavored cooking spray. Bake 35-40 minutes or until knife inserted in center comes out clean. Let stand 5-10 minutes before serving.

Serves 4
Each serving equals:
HE: 1 3/4 Pr (1/2 limited), 1 1/4 Ve, 1 1/4 Br
236 Calories, 9 gm Fa, 15 gm Pr, 24 gm Ca, 437 mg So
Diabetic: 2 Mt, 1 Ve, 1 St

TOMATOES WITH MOZZARELLA

2 cups diced fresh tomatoes
1 1/2 oz shredded reduced fat Mozzarella cheese
(1/3 cup)
3 Tablespoons fat free Italian dressing
(4 calories per Tablespoon)
2 teaspoons dried basil

In medium bowl combine tomatoes, cheese, Italian dressing and basil. Mix gently to combine. Cover and chill.

Serves 4 (full l/2 cup)
Each serving equals:
HE: 1 Ve, 1/2 Pr, 3 OC
48 Calories, 2 gm Fa, 4 gm Pr, 4 gm Ca, 186 Mg So
Diabetic: 1/2 Ve

FRIED TOMATOES WITH MUSHROOM SAUCE

6 Tablespoons flour

1/4 teaspoon lemon pepper

4 fresh medium red tomatoes, sliced

1 Tablespoon + 1 teaspoon reduced
    calorie margarine

1 can Campbell's Healthy Request
    Cream of Mushroom soup

1 Tablespoon fresh basil, chopped
    or 1 teaspoon dried basil

In saucer combine flour and lemon pepper. Dip tomato slices in flour mixture. Melt margarine in large skillet. Place tomato slices in skillet. Cook tomatoes over low heat until lightly browned on both sides. Remove to heated platter. Stir soup and basil into skillet. Heat. Pour sauce over tomatoes.

Serves 6
Each serving equals:
HE: 2/3 Ve, 1/3 Br, 1/3 Fa, 28 OC
81 Calories, 2 gm Fa, 2 gmPr, 14 gm Ca, 229 mg So
Diabetic: 1 Ve, 1/2 St, 1/2 Fa

TOMATO PIE

1 purchased 9" unbaked refrigerated pie crust
4 fresh medium red tomatoes, peeled and sliced
1/2 cup fat free mayonnaise
    (8 calories per Tablespoon)
2 teaspoons Worcestershire sauce
2 teaspoons Sprinkle Sweet
6 oz shredded reduced fat Cheddar cheese (1 1/2 cups)
1 Tablespoon dried parsley flakes

Preheat oven to 450 degrees. Place pie crust in 9" pie plate. Flute edges. Bake until crust is light brown, BUT not done, about 6 minutes. Remove from oven. Lower heat to 350 degrees. Place a layer of sliced tomatoes in pie crust. In small bowl combine mayonnaise, Worcestershire sauce, Sprinkle Sweet and cheese. Spread 1/3 of mixture over tomatoes, cover with more tomatoes and repeat until 3 layers of each are in pie crust. Top with parsley flakes. Bake 30 minutes. Let cool 2-3 minutes before cutting.

Serves 8
Each serving equals:
HE: 1 Pr, 1/2 Br, 1/2 Ve, 1/2 Sl, 18 OC
195 Calories, 10 gm Fa, 7 gm Pr, 19 gm Ca, 445 mg So
Diabetic: 1 Mt, 1 St, 1 Fa, 1/2 Ve

TOMATO—POTATO—ZUCCHINI PIE

Crust:
10 oz shredded frozen potatoes, slightly thawed
    (full 3 cups)
1/2 cup diced onion
1 egg, beaten or equivalent in egg substitute
3 Tablespoons flour
1/2 teaspoon parsley flakes

Filling:
6 oz shredded reduced fat Swiss cheese (1 1/2 cups)
2 cups thinly sliced zucchini
2 cups sliced fresh tomatoes
1 teaspoon basil
1/2 teaspoon garlic powder
1 teaspoon oregano
1/4 teaspoon lemon pepper
1/2 cup diced onion

Preheat oven to 350 degrees. In medium bowl combine potatoes, onion, egg, flour and parsley flakes. Mix well. Pat mixture into a 9" pie pan sprayed with olive flavored cooking spray. Bake 30 minutes or until crust turns lightly browned. Layer half the cheese on crust. Arrange zucchini over cheese. Place tomato slices on top of zucchini. Sprinkle basil, garlic powder, oregano, lemon pepper and onions over tomatoes. Top with remaining cheese. Bake 45 minutes or until top is brown.

Serves 6
Each serving equals:
HE: 1 1/2 Pr, 1 1/2 Ve, 1/2 Br
203 Calories, 8 gm Fa, 10 gm Pr, 23 gm Ca, 463 mg So
Diabetic: 1 Mt, 1 Ve, 1 St, 1 Fa

HINT: Mr. Dell's shredded potatoes work great.

SCALLOPED TOMATOES

3/4 cup chopped onion
1/4 cup chopped green bell pepper
3 cups canned tomatoes, coarsely chopped, with juice
1 Tablespoon prepared mustard
1 Tablespoon Brown Sugar Twin
3 oz dry bread crumbs (3/4 cup)
1 teaspoon Taco seasoning mix
3 oz shredded reduced fat Cheddar cheese (3/4 cup)

Preheat oven to 350 degrees. In large skillet sprayed with butter flavored cooking spray, saute onion and green pepper until tender. Add tomatoes with juice. Stir in mustard and Brown Sugar Twin. Add bread crumbs, taco seasoning and cheese. Mix well. Pour into 8 x 8 baking dish sprayed with butter flavored cooking spray. Bake 30-35 minutes.

Serves 4
Each serving equals:
HE: 2 Ve, 1 Pr, 1 Br, 1 OC
196 Calories, 5 gm Fa, 11 gm Pr, 27 gm Ca, 693 mg So
Diabetic: 2 Ve, 1 Mt, 1 St

CHEESY VEGETABLE SAUTE

1 Tablespoon + 1 teaspoon reduced
    calorie margarine
1 cup green bell pepper strips
1 cup red onion, cut into rings
1 teaspoon minced garlic
1/2 teaspoon dried basil
2 medium tomatoes,
    peeled and cut into wedges
3 oz shredded reduced fat Mozzarella cheese(3/4 cup)

In large skillet melt margarine. Add peppers, onions, garlic and basil. Saute until vegetables are crisp-tender. Stir in tomatoes. Sprinkle cheese over top. Cover and continue cooking until cheese is melted, about 3 minutes. Serve immediately.

Serves 4
Each serving equals:
HE: 1 1/2 Ve, 1 Pr, 1/2 Fa
95 Calories, 4 gm Fa, 7 gm Pr, 7 gm Ca, 243 mg So
Diabetic: 1 Ve, 1 Mt, 1/2 Fa

ITALIAN POTATO VEGETABLE BAKE

15 oz raw potatoes, thickly sliced (3 cups)
1 (16 oz) pkg frozen California blend vegetables
1/2 cup canned sliced mushrooms, drained
2 teaspoons Italian seasoning
1/8 teaspoon pepper
1 3/4 cups Hunt's Chunky Tomato Sauce
3 oz shredded reduced fat Mozzarella cheese (3/4 cup)

Preheat oven to 350 degrees. In medium saucepan cook potatoes and vegetable blend in water until potatoes are almost tender. Drain. Spray 8 x 8 baking dish with butter flavored cooking spray. In a medium bowl combine potatoes and vegetable mixture with mushrooms, Italian seasoning and pepper. Pour into baking dish. Evenly pour tomato sauce over top. Sprinkle cheese over tomato sauce. Bake 30 minutes.

Serves 4
Each serving equals:
HE: 3 1/2 Ve, 1 Pr, 3/4 Br,
211 Calories, 5 gm Fa, 11 gm Pr, 31 gm Ca, 937 mg So
Diabetic: 3 Ve, 1 St, 1 Mt

HINT: 1) 1 cup frozen carrots, 1 cup frozen cauliflower and 1 cup frozen broccoli can be used instead of California blend.
2) 4 oz diced cooked chicken breast (scant 1 cup) can be added.

MAIN DISHES

K. Blitz
8/41

MAIN DISHES

FETTUCCINE ALFREDO

2 cups hot cooked fettuccine
2 Tablespoons + 2 teaspoons reduced
   calorie margarine
3 oz grated Parmesan cheese (1 cup)
1/2 cup evaporated skim milk

Place hot fettuccine in a large bowl. Add margarine, Parmesan cheese and evaporated skim milk. Toss gently to combine. Serve at once.

Serves 4 (2/3 cup)
Each serving equals:
HE: 1 Br, 1 Fa, 1 Pr, 1/4 SM
251 Calories, 10 gm Fa, 15 gm Pr, 24 gm Ca, 471 mg So
Diabetic: 1 1/2 St, 1 Fa, 1 Mt

FESTIVE NOODLES WITH POPPY SEEDS

1/2 cup frozen peas
1 1/2 cups hot cooked noodles
1 Tablespoon + 1 teaspoon reduced calorie margarine
1 teaspoon poppy seeds
1/8 teaspoon pepper

In medium saucepan combine peas and noodles. Add margarine, poppy seeds and pepper. Toss gently to combine. Cook over medium heat until heated through, stirring often.

Serves 4 (1/2 cup)
Each serving equals:
HE: 1 Br, 1/2 Fa, 4 OC
104 Calories, 2 gm Fa, 4 gm Pr, 17 gm Ca, 41 mg So
Diabetic: 1 St, 1/2 Fa

CHEESY MACARONI VEGETABLE BAKE

2 cups cooked elbow macaroni
2 cups frozen California Blend vegetables,
    cooked and drained
2/3 cup non fat dry milk powder
1 cup water
1 Tablespoon Dijon mustard
3 oz shredded reduced fat Cheddar cheese (3/4 cup)
3 oz shredded reduced fat Mozzarella cheese (3/4 cup)
1/8 teaspoon lemon pepper

Preheat oven to 350 degrees. In large bowl combine macaroni and vegetables. In small bowl combine dry milk powder and water. Add to macaroni mixture. Stir in mustard, Cheddar and Mozzarella cheeses and pepper. Mix well to combine. Spray an 8x8 baking dish with butter flavored cooking spray. Pour mixture into dish. Bake 30 minutes.

Serves 4
Each serving equals:
HE: 2 Pr, 1 Br, 1 Ve, 1/2 SM
274 Calories, 7 gm Fa, 21 gm Pr, 31 gm Ca, 569 mg So
Diabetic: 2 Mt, 1 St, 1 Ve, 1/2 SM

HINT: 1 cup frozen carrots, 1/2 cup frozen cauliflower, and 1/2 cup frozen broccoli can be used in place of California Blend vegetables.

CREAMY POTATO and HAM BAKE

15 oz frozen shredded potatoes, thawed (4 1/2 cups)
1 1/2 cups frozen peas
6 oz diced Dubuque 97% fat free ham (full 1 cup)
1 Tablespoon flour
1/2 teaspoon dried parsley flakes
1/4 teaspoon pepper
1 can Campbell's Healthy Request
   Cream of Mushroom soup

Preheat oven to 350 degrees. In large bowl combine potatoes, peas and ham. In a small bowl combine flour, parsley, pepper and soup. Pour soup mixture over potato mixture. Mix well to combine. Pour into 8x8 baking dish sprayed with butter flavored cooking spray. Bake 25-30 minutes.

Serves 6
Each serving equals:
HE: 1 Br, 2/3 Pr, 33 OC
139 Calories, 2 gm Fa, 8 gm Pr, 22 gm Ca, 496 mg So
Diabetic: 1 1/2 St, 1 Mt

HINT: Mr. Dell's shredded potatoes work great.

PARTY POTATOES

25 oz frozen shredded potatoes, thawed (8 cups)
1 cup canned sliced mushrooms, drained
3 Tablespoons dried onion flakes
1 1/2 cups evaporated skim milk
1/3 cup nonfat dry milk powder
3 Tablespoons flour
1 teaspoon dried parsley flakes
1/8 teaspoon pepper
6 oz shredded reduced fat Cheddar cheese (1 1/2 cups)

Spray an 8x12 baking dish with butter flavored cooking spray. In a large bowl combine potatoes, mushrooms, and dried onion flakes. In small bowl combine evaporated skim milk, dry milk powder, flour, parsley flakes and pepper. Add to potato mixture. Mix well to combine. Pour into baking dish. Top with cheese. Cover and let set in refrigerator for at least one hour. Bake 30 minutes in a 350 degree oven.

Serves 8
Each serving equals:
HE: 1 Pr, 3/4 Br, 1/2 SM, 1/4 Ve
185 Calories, 3 gm Fa, 13 gm Pr, 27 gm Ca, 325 mg So
Diabetic: 2 St, 1 Mt

HINT: Mr. Dell's shredded potatoes work great.

97

RIO GRANDE POTATOES

20 oz unpeeled baking potatoes, thickly sliced (4 cups)
8 oz ground turkey or beef (90% lean)
1 cup chunky salsa
1/4 cup fat free sour cream
    (15 calories per Tablespoon)
2 1/4 oz shredded reduced fat Cheddar,
    Monterey Jack or Taco cheese (full 1/2 cup)

Preheat oven to 350 degrees. Place potatoes in 8x8 baking dish. Spray potatoes with butter flavored cooking spray. Bake until tender about 30-45 minutes. In skillet sprayed with olive flavored cooking spray brown meat. Stir in salsa. Lower heat. Simmer, uncovered until potatoes are done. When serving place 1/4 of potatoes on each serving plate. Spoon meat mixture evenly over potatoes. Top each with 1 Tablespoon sour cream and about 2 Tablespoons cheese.

Serves 4
Each serving equals:
HE: 2 1/4 Pr, 1 Br, 1/2 Ve, 15 OC
255 Calories, 7 gm Fa, 19 gm Pr, 29 gm Ca, 440 mg So
Diabetic: 2 Mt, 2 St

MEXICAN RICE

1/2 cup chopped onion
2 cups chunky salsa
1/8 teaspoon pepper
2 cups cooked rice
3 3/4 oz shredded reduced fat Cheddar cheese
    (scant 1 cup)

Preheat oven to 350 degrees. In skillet sprayed with olive flavored cooking spray saute onion until tender. Add salsa and pepper. Mix in rice and 3/4 cup cheese. Stir until cheese is melted. Pour into 8x8 baking dish sprayed with olive flavored cooking spray. Bake 15 minutes. Sprinkle remaining cheese on top and bake additional 5 minutes or until cheese melts.

Serves 4
Each serving equals:
HE: 1 1/4 Pr, 1 1/4 Ve, 1 Br
149 Calories, 3 gm Fa, 9 gm Pr, 21 gm Ca, 655 mg So
Diabetic: 1 Mt, 1 Ve, 1 St

ORIENTAL RICE WITH VEGETABLES

1/2 cup sliced fresh mushrooms
2 teaspoons reduced calorie margarine
2 cups Campbell's Healthy Request chicken broth
1/4 cup sliced green onion
1/2 cup diagonally sliced celery
1/4 cup red bell pepper strips
1/2 cup bean sprouts
1 Tablespoon reduced sodium soy sauce
4 oz uncooked instant rice (1 1/3 cups)

In medium sauce pan saute mushrooms in margarine. Add chicken broth. Bring mixture to a boil. Add onion, celery, red pepper, bean sprouts and soy sauce. Stir in rice. Cover. Remove from heat. Let stand 5 minutes or until all liquid is absorbed. Fluff with fork before serving.

Serves 4 (full 3/4 cup)
Each serving equals:
HE: 1 Br, 1 Ve, 1/4 Fa, 8 OC
133 Calories, 1 gm Fa, 4 gm Pr, 27 gm Ca, 270 mg So
Diabetic: 1 1/2 St, 1 Ve

RICE PRIMAVERA

1 Tablespoon + 1 teaspoon reduced calorie margarine
2 cups Campbell's Healthy Request chicken broth
1 teaspoon dried basil leaves
1/2 cup finely chopped onion
1 cup frozen sliced carrots
1 cup frozen green beans
4 oz uncooked instant rice (1 1/3 cups)
1 1/2 oz grated Parmesan cheese (1/2 cup)

In medium saucepan combine margarine, chicken broth, basil, onion, carrots and green beans. Bring mixture to a boil. Cover and simmer until vegetables are tender, about 10 minutes. Stir in rice. Cover. Remove from heat. Let stand 5 minutes or until all broth is absorbed. Stir in Parmesan cheese and fluff with a fork before serving.

Serves 4 (full 1 cup)
Each serving equals:
HE: 1 1/4 Ve, 1 Br, 1/2 Pr, 1/2 Fa, 8 OC
204 Calories, 5 gm Fa, 9 gm Pr, 31 gm Ca, 463 mg So
Diabetic: 1 1/2 St, 1 Ve, 1/2 Mt, 1/2 Fa

FRIED RICE WITH HAM

2 eggs, beaten or equivalent in egg substitute
1 teaspoon vegetable oil
3 oz diced ham (90% lean) (1/2 cup)
1/4 cup sliced green onion
1/4 cup shredded carrot
1/4 cup frozen peas, thawed
1 3/4 cups cooked rice
4 teaspoons reduced sodium soy sauce
1/8 teaspoon pepper

Place eggs in skillet or wok sprayed with butter flavored cooking spray. Using a spatula lift eggs as they cook, letting uncooked part run underneath until set. Transfer eggs to cutting board and cut into shreds. Pour vegetable oil into skillet or wok set on medium high heat. Add ham, onion, carrots and peas. Stir fry about 1 minute. Add shredded eggs, rice, soy sauce and pepper, stirring until heated through.

Serves 4 (3/4 cup)
Each serving equals:
HE: 1 1/4 Pr (1/2 limited), 1 Br, 1/4 Fa, 1/4 Ve
151 Calories, 6 gm Fa, 9 gm Pr, 15 gm Ca, 232 mg So
Diabetic: 1 Mt, 1 St

HINT: Carl Buddig ham works great.

SOUTH OF THE BORDER BEANS

20 oz canned Great Northern beans,
    rinsed and drained
3/4 cup chunky salsa
1 Tablespoon catsup
1 Tablespoon Brown Sugar Twin
1/2 teaspoon dried parsley flakes
1/8 teaspoon pepper
3 oz shredded reduced fat Cheddar cheese (3/4 cup)

Preheat oven to 350 degrees. In medium saucepan warm beans. Add salsa and catsup. Mix in Brown Sugar Twin, parsley and pepper. Add cheese. Mix well to combine. Pour into 8x8 baking dish sprayed with olive flavored cooking spray. Bake 20-30 minutes.

Serves 6
Each serving equals:
HE: 2 1/3 Pr, 1/4 Ve, 4 OC
155 Calories, 2 gm Fa, 12 gm Pr, 22 gm Ca, 260 mg So
Diabetic: 1 1/2 St, 1 Mt

HINT: 2 (16 oz) cans of beans usually is 20 oz drained
      weight

CREAMY CORN SCALLOP

1 can Campbell's Healthy Request
    Cream of Mushroom soup
2 Tablespoons dried onion flakes
1/2 teaspoon dry mustard
1/8 teaspoon pepper
2 teaspoons Sprinkle Sweet
2 cups canned whole kernel corn, drained
3 1/2 oz Ritz crackers, crumbled (1 3/4 cups)

Preheat oven to 400 degrees. In medium bowl combine soup, onion, mustard, pepper and Sprinkle Sweet. Mix in corn and cracker crumbs. Pour into an 8x8 baking dish sprayed with butter flavored cooking spray. Bake 25 minutes.

Serves 6
Each serving equals:
HE: 1 1/3 Br, 1/2 Sl, 8 OC
159 Calories, 5 gm Fa, 3 gm Pr, 25 gm Ca, 527 mg So
Diabetic: 1 1/2 St, 1 Fa

ALL AMERICAN CASSEROLE

8 oz ground turkey or beef (90% lean)
1/2 cup chopped onion
10 oz frozen shredded potatoes, thawed (3 full cups)
2 cups canned sliced carrots, drained
1 3/4 cups Hunt's Chunky Tomato Sauce
1/8 teaspoon lemon pepper
1 teaspoon dried basil or 1 Tablespoon
    finely chopped fresh basil
1 cup frozen peas
3 oz shredded reduced fat Cheddar cheese
    (3/4 cup)

Preheat oven to 350 degrees. In skillet sprayed with butter flavored cooking spray saute meat and onion until browned. In large mixing bowl combine potatoes, carrots, tomato sauce, lemon pepper and basil. Mix in meat mixture, peas and cheese. Pour into 8x8 baking dish sprayed with butter flavored cooking spray. Bake 20-30 minutes or until cheese is melted through.

Serves 4
Each serving equals:
HE: 3 Ve, 2 1/4 Pr, 1 Br
281 Calories, 9 gm Fa, 20 gm Pr, 31 gm Ca, 1002 mg So
Diabetic: 2 Mt, 2 Ve, 1 1/2 St

HINT: Mr. Dell's shredded potatoes work great.

BARBEQUE BISCUIT CUPS

8 oz ground turkey or beef (90% lean)
1/4 cup chopped green bell pepper
1/4 cup finely chopped onion
1 cup tomato sauce
1 Tablespoon Brown Sugar Twin
1 teaspoon prepared mustard
1/8 teaspoon pepper
1 (7.5 oz) can flaky refrigerator biscuits
2 1/4 oz shredded reduced fat Cheddar cheese
   (full 1/2 cup)

Preheat oven to 400 degrees. In large skillet sprayed with olive flavored cooking spray brown ground meat, green pepper and onions. Add tomato sauce, Brown Sugar Twin, mustard and pepper. Simmer 5 minutes. Place each biscuit in an ungreased muffin cup, pressing dough up sides to edge of cup. Evenly spoon meat mixture into cups. Bake 10-15 minutes or until golden brown. Sprinkle with cheese and continue to bake 2-3 minutes or until cheese melts.

Serves 5 (2 cups each)
Each serving equals:
HE: 1 1/2 Br, 1 1/2 Pr, 1 Ve, 1 OC
270 Calories, 10 gm Fa, 16 gm Pr, 25 gm Ca, 873 mg So
Diabetic: 1 1/2 St, 1 1/2 Mt, 1 Ve

CABBAGE AND RICE CASSEROLE

8 oz ground turkey or beef (90% lean)
2 cups coarsely chopped cabbage
1/2 cup chopped onion
2 oz uncooked regular rice (2/3 cup)
3 cups canned tomatoes, chopped fine, with juice
2 teaspoons prepared mustard
2 Tablespoons Brown Sugar Twin
1/8 teaspoon lemon pepper

Preheat oven to 350 degrees. In large skillet sprayed with butter flavored cooking spray brown meat. Spray an 8x8 baking dish with butter flavored cooking spray. Layer cabbage on bottom of dish. Cover with onion, browned meat and rice. In a small bowl combine chopped tomatoes with juice, mustard, Brown Sugar Twin and lemon pepper. Pour tomato mixture over rice. Cover and bake 1 1/2 hours. Uncover and bake additional 10 minutes.

Serves 4
Each serving equals:
HE: 2 3/4 Ve, 1 1/2 Pr, 1/2 Br, 2 OC
193 Calories, 5 gm Fa, 14 gm Pr, 23 gm Ca, 390 mg So
Diabetic: 1 1/2 Mt, 1 Ve, 1 St

CHILI JACKPOT CASSEROLE

8 oz ground turkey or beef (90% lean)
1/4 cup chopped green bell pepper
1/4 cup chopped onion
1 1/2 teaspoons chili seasoning mix
1/4 teaspoon pepper
1 3/4 cups Hunt's Chunky Tomato Sauce
3 cups cooked rotini macaroni
10 oz canned red kidney beans, rinsed and drained
3 3/4 oz shredded reduced fat Cheddar cheese
(scant 1 cup)

Preheat oven to 350 degrees. In large skillet sprayed with olive flavored cooking spray brown meat, green pepper and onion. Add chili seasoning mix and pepper. Mix well. Stir in tomato sauce, cooked rotini macaroni, kidney beans and half of the cheese. Mix well to combine. Pour into 8x8 baking dish sprayed with olive flavored cooking spray. Sprinkle remaining cheese over top. Bake 20 minutes or until cheese melts.

Serves 6
Each serving equals:
HE: 2 2/3 Pr, 1 1/3 Ve, 1 Br
261 Calories, 7 gm Fa, 19 gm Pr, 31 gm Ca, 583 mg So
Diabetic: 2 Mt, 2 St

HINT: A 16 oz can of red kidney beans usually is
10 oz drained weight

DEEP DISH PIZZA

16 oz ground turkey or beef (90% lean)
1/2 cup chopped onion
1 teaspoon dried parsley flakes
1/4 teaspoon minced garlic
3 cups Bisquick reduced fat baking mix
3/4 cup water
1 1/2 teaspoons pizza spice or Italian seasoning
1 3/4 cups tomato sauce
1 cup canned sliced mushrooms, drained
1 cup chopped green bell pepper
6 oz shredded reduced fat Mozzarella
    cheese (1 1/2 cups)

Preheat oven to 425 degrees. In large skillet sprayed with olive flavored cooking spray brown meat and onion. Add parsley flakes and garlic. Spray jelly roll pan with olive flavored cooking spray. In large bowl combine baking mix and water until soft ball is formed. Place dough on wax paper and knead 20 times. Pat dough in bottom of pan and up sides. Add Italian seasoning to tomato sauce. Spread sauce over dough. Spoon meat mixture over sauce. Top with mushrooms, green pepper and cheese. Bake 20 minutes.

Serves 12
Each serving equals:
HE: 1 2/3 Pr, 1 1/3 Br, 1 Ve
214 Calories, 8 gm Fa, 14 gm Pr, 22 gm Ca, 568 mg So
2 Mt, 1 St, 1 Ve, 1 Free Ve

IMPOSSIBLE LASAGNA

8 oz ground turkey or beef (90% lean)
1/2 cup fat free cottage cheese
3/4 oz Parmesan cheese (1/4 cup)
2 teaspoons Italian seasoning
1 cup tomato sauce
3 oz shredded reduced fat Mozzarella cheese
   (3/4 cup)
1 cup skim milk
1/3 cup nonfat dry milk powder
9 Tablespoons Bisquick reduced fat baking mix
2 eggs or equivalent in egg substitute
1/2 teaspoon salt
1/8 teaspoon pepper

Preheat oven to 400 degrees. In large skillet sprayed with olive flavored cooking spray brown meat. Spray an 8x8 baking dish with olive flavored cooking spray. Layer cottage cheese and Parmesan cheese on bottom. Add Italian seasoning, tomato sauce and half the mozzarella cheese to browned meat. Spoon over cheese layer. In a blender combine skim milk, dry milk powder, baking mix, eggs, salt and pepper for 15 seconds on high speed. Pour over meat mixture. Bake 30 minutes. Spread remaining cheese on top and bake additional 5 minutes. Let set 5 minutes before cutting.

Serves 6
Each serving equals:
HE: 2 1/3 Pr (1/3 limited), 2/3 Ve, 1/2 Br, 1/3 SM
229 Calories, 9 gm Fa, 21 gm Pr, 15 gm Ca, 752 mg So
Diabetic: 3 Mt, 1 St

MEXICALLI PIE

16 oz ground turkey or beef (90% lean)
1/2 cup chopped onion
1/2 cup chopped green and/or red bell peppers
1 1/2 cups frozen corn
1 cup chunky salsa
3 oz shredded reduced fat Cheddar or Monterey Jack
    cheese (3/4 cup)
1/8 teaspoon pepper
3 oz crushed corn chips (1 cup)

Preheat oven to 350 degrees. In large skillet sprayed with olive flavored cooking spray brown meat, onions and green pepper. Add corn, salsa, cheese, and pepper. Spray a 10" pie plate with olive flavored cooking spray. Place meat mixture in pie plate. Top with crushed corn chips. Bake 30 minutes. Cool 10 minutes before serving.

Serves 8
Each serving equals:
HE: 2 Pr, 3/4 Br, 1/2 Ve, 30 OC
204 Calories, 10 gm Fa, 15 gm Pr, 14 gm Ca, 324 mg So
Diabetic: 2 Mt, 1 St

MEATLOAF WITH VEGETABLE STUFFING

1/2 cup canned sliced mushrooms, drained
1 cup canned carrots, drained and chopped
1 cup canned green beans, drained and chopped
3/4 oz dried bread crumbs (3 Tablespoons)
2 eggs or equivalent in egg substitute
16 oz ground turkey or beef (90% lean)
1/2 cup chopped onion
1 1/2 oz rolled oats (1/2 cup)
1 Tablespoon Worcestershire sauce
1/4 cup catsup
1/4 teaspoon pepper
1/2 teaspoon garlic powder

Preheat oven to 375 degrees. In medium bowl combine mushrooms, carrots, green beans, bread crumbs and 1 egg. Set aside. In large bowl combine meat, onion, oats, remaining egg, Worcestershire sauce, catsup, pepper and garlic powder. Spread half of meat mixture in bottom of ungreased 9 x 5 loaf pan. Cover with vegetable mixture, spreading evenly. Spread remaining meat mixture over vegetables. Bake 45-55 minutes. Cool 10 minutes before serving.

Serves 6
Each serving equals:
HE: 2 1/3 Pr (1/3 limited), 1 Ve, 1/2 Br, 10 OC
211 Calories, 9 gm Fa, 18 gm Pr, 15 gm Ca, 442 mg So
Diabetic: 2 Mt, 1 Ve, 1 St

MEAT ROLL

8 oz ground turkey or beef (90% lean)
1/2 cup finely chopped onion
1/2 cup diced green bell pepper
3/4 cup Bisquick reduced fat baking mix
3 Tablespoons skim milk
2 1/4 oz shredded reduced fat Cheddar cheese
    (full 1/2 cup)
1 3/4 cups Hunt's Chunky Tomato Sauce
2 Tablespoons Brown Sugar Twin
1/4 teaspoon pepper
1 Tablespoon chopped fresh parsley
    or 1 teaspoon dried parsley

Preheat oven to 400 degrees. Spray a 9x13" baking sheet with butter flavored cooking spray. In a skillet sprayed with butter flavored cooking spray brown meat, onions and green pepper. In medium bowl blend baking mix and milk to form a soft dough. Place between waxed paper and roll into rectangle 6"x9". Cover with meat mixture. Top with cheese. Roll as for jelly roll. Place on prepared baking sheet, seam side down. Slash top several times. Bake 15-20 minutes. When almost done, spray top with butter flavored cooking spray. Meanwhile, place tomato sauce in medium saucepan. Add Brown Sugar Twin, pepper and parsley. Simmer until meat roll is done. Cut roll into 4 pieces. Top each piece with about 1/2 cup sauce.

Serves 4
Each serving equals:
HE: 2 1/4 Pr, 2 1/4 Ve, 1 Br, 7 OC
269 Calories, 10 gm Fa, 18 gm Pr, 27 gm Ca, 1039 mg So
Diabetic: 2 Mt, 2 Ve, 1 St

PIZZA CASSEROLE

8 oz ground turkey or beef (90% lean)
1/2 cup chopped onion
3 cups cooked noodles
2 oz thinly sliced pepperoni, chopped (full 1/3 cup)
1 3/4 cups Hunt's Chunky Tomato Sauce
1 cup canned sliced mushrooms, drained
1 teaspoon pizza spice or Italian seasoning
3 oz shredded reduced fat Mozzarella cheese
    (3/4 cup)

Preheat oven to 350 degrees. In large skillet sprayed with olive flavored cooking spray brown meat and onion. Stir in noodles, pepperoni, tomato sauce mushrooms and seasoning. Mix well. Pour into ungreased 8x8 baking dish. Bake 20 minutes. Sprinkle top with cheese. Bake an additional 5 minutes or until cheese melts.

Serves 6
Each serving equals:
HE: 2 Pr (1/3 limited), 1 2/3 Ve, 1 Br
282 Calories, 11 gm Fa, 18 gm Pr, 28 gm Ca, 893 mg So
Diabetic: 2 Mt, 2 Ve, 1 St

SALISBURY STEAK

1 1/2 oz dried bread crumbs (6 Tablespoons)
8 oz ground turkey or beef (90% lean)
1 egg or equivalent in egg substitute
1/8 teaspoon pepper
1/2 cup chopped onion
2 Tablespoons Worcestershire sauce
3 Tablespoons catsup
1 can Campbell's Healthy Request
    Cream of Mushroom soup

Preheat oven to 350 degrees. In medium bowl combine bread crumbs, meat, egg, pepper and onion. Form into 4 patties. Place in skillet sprayed with butter flavored cooking spray. Brown patties on both sides. Place browned patties in 8x8 baking dish. In small bowl combine Worcestershire sauce, catsup and soup. Pour over patties. Bake 30 minutes.

Serves 4
Each serving equals:
HE: 1 3/4 Pr (1/4 limited), 1/2 Br, 1/4 Ve, 1/2 Sl, 13 OC
210 Calories, 8 gm Fa, 14 gm Pr, 20 gm Ca, 697 mg So
Diabetic: 2 Mt, 1 St

SLOPPY JOE TURNOVERS

8 oz ground turkey or beef (90% lean)
1/2 cup chopped onion
1/2 cup chopped green bell pepper
1 cup tomato sauce
1 Tablespoon Brown Sugar Twin
1/8 teaspoon garlic powder
1/2 teaspoon Worcestershire sauce
1 (8 serving) can Crescent refrigerated rolls

Preheat oven to 375 degrees. In large skillet sprayed with olive flavored cooking spray brown meat, onion and green pepper. Add tomato sauce, Brown Sugar Twin, garlic powder and Worcestershire sauce. Simmer 5 minutes. Separate crescent roll dough into 8 triangles. Lay triangles on large ungreased cookie sheet. Place about 1 Tablespoon of meat mixture in center of each triangle. Bring 3 corners together in center of each triangle. Bake for 12 to 16 minutes or until golden brown. Remove from oven and quickly spray tops with butter flavored cooking spray.

Serves 8
Each serving equals:
HE: 1 Br, 3/4 Pr, 3/4 Ve
155 Calories, 8 gm Fa, 7 gm Pr, 14 gm Ca, 446 mg So
Diabetic: 1 St, 1 Mt, 1/2 Fa

TACO CASSEROLE

8 oz ground turkey or beef (90% lean)
1/2 cup chopped onion
1/2 cup chopped green bell pepper
1 3/4 cups Hunt's Chunky Tomato Sauce
1 Tablespoon taco seasoning mix
2 cups cooked noodles
3 oz shredded reduced fat Taco or Cheddar cheese
(3/4 cup)

Preheat oven to 350 degrees. In large skillet sprayed with olive flavored cooking spray, brown meat, onion and green pepper. Add tomato sauce and taco seasoning. Simmer 5 - 10 minutes. Stir in cooked noodles. Pour into 8x8 baking dish sprayed with olive flavored cooking spray. Bake 15-20 minutes. Top with cheese and bake another 10 minutes or until cheese melts. Let set 5 minutes before serving.

Serves 4
Each serving equals:
HE: 2 1/2 Pr, 2 1/4 Ve, 1 Br
295 Calories, 10 gm Fa, 21 gm Pr, 31 gm Ca, 828 mg So
Diabetic: 2 Mt, 2 Ve, 1 St

HINT: If you like your tacos hotter, use more taco
seasoning.

TAMALE PIE

1 1/2 cups water
4 teaspoons reduced calorie margarine
1 (6 serving) pkg cornbread stuffing mix
8 oz ground turkey or beef (90% lean)
1/2 cup chopped green bell pepper
1/2 cup chopped onion
1 oz sliced black olives (1/4 cup)
1 3/4 cups Hunt's Chunky Tomato Sauce
2 teaspoons chili seasoning mix
3 oz shredded reduced fat Taco or Cheddar cheese
    (3/4 cup)

Preheat oven to 350 degrees. In medium saucepan combine water and margarine in saucepan. Bring mixture to a boil. Simmer 5 minutes. Add dry cornbread mix. Mix well to combine. In large skillet sprayed with olive flavored cooking spray brown meat, green pepper and onion. Add olives, tomato sauce and chili seasoning. Stir in cheese. Mix well to combine. Pour into 8x8 baking dish.Spread prepared stuffing mix on top of meat mixture. Bake 20-25 minutes.

Serves 6
Each serving equals:
HE: 1 2/3 Pr, 1 1/2 Ve, 1 Br, 1/2 Fa, 30 OC
253 Calories, 9 gm Fa, 15 gm Pr, 29 gm Ca, 954 mg So
Diabetic: 2 Ve, 1 1/2 Mt, 1 St, 1/2 Fa

HINT: Stove Top Stuffing works great.

ROAST BEEF ROLLS

1 cup minced fresh mushrooms
1 cup finely diced onion
1 Tablespoon + 1 teaspoon reduced calorie margarine
8 slices cold lean roast beef, sliced very thin
    (approximately 1/2 oz each)
1/4 cup fat free 1000 Island dressing
    (20 calories or less per Tablespoon)

Preheat oven to 350 degrees. In medium skillet saute mushrooms and onion in margarine until lightly browned. Spread roast beef slices with mushroom and onion filling. Roll each slice of beef and place seam side down in 8x12 baking dish sprayed with butter flavored cooking spray. Spoon dressing evenly over beef rolls. Bake 10 minutes or until rolls are heated through. Serve immediately.

Serves 4 (2 each)
Each serving equals:
HE: 1 Pr, 1 Ve, 1/2 Fa, 20 OC
100 Calories, 3 gm Fa, 9 gm Pr, 9 gm Ca, 167 mg So
Diabetic: 1 Mt, 1 Ve

HINT: Purchase roast beef from deli and have them
        slice it for you.

119

POTATOES OLE'

1/2 cup chopped onions
10 oz frozen shredded potatoes, thawed (3 full cups)
1 cup canned sliced carrots, drained
1 cup canned sliced green beans, drained
1 can Campbell's Healthy Request
   Cream of Mushroom soup
1 cup chunky salsa
4 oz diced lean roast beef (scant 1 cup)
3 oz shredded reduced fat Cheddar cheese (3/4 cup)
1/2 teaspoon lemon pepper

Preheat oven to 350 degrees. In skillet sprayed with olive flavored cooking spray brown onions. Add potatoes, carrots, green beans, soup, salsa, beef, cheese and lemon pepper. Mix well. Spray an 8x8 baking dish with olive flavored cooking spray. Pour mixture into dish. Bake 45 minutes.

Serves 4
Each serving equals:
HE: 2 Pr, 1 3/4 Ve, 1/2 Br, 1/2 Sl, 1 OC
232 Calories, 6 gm Fa, 18 gm Pr, 26 gm Ca, 1043 mg So
Diabetic: 2 Mt, 2 Ve, 1 St

HINT: 1) Purchase chunk of roast beef from deli and dice it when you get home.
      2) Mr. Dell's shredded potatoes work great

CHICKEN POT CASSEROLE

2 cups cooked noodles
1/2 cup chopped onion
6 oz diced cooked chicken breast (full 1 cup)
1 cup frozen carrots, thawed
1 cup frozen green beans, thawed
1/2 cup frozen peas, thawed
1/2 cup canned sliced mushrooms, drained
1 can Campbell's Healthy Request
    Cream of Mushroom soup
1/2 teaspoon poultry seasoning
1/8 teaspoon pepper
1 teaspoon dried parsley flakes
1 1/2 oz shredded reduced fat Cheddar
    cheese (1/3 cup)
3/4 oz dried bread crumbs (3 Tablespoons)

Preheat oven to 350 degrees. In large bowl combine noodles, onion, chicken, carrots, green beans, peas, mushrooms, soup, poultry seasoning, pepper and parsley. Pour into ungreased 8x8 baking dish. Bake 15-20 minutes or until hot. Sprinkle cheese and bread crumbs on top and bake additional 5 minutes or until cheese melts.

Serves 4
Each serving equals:
HE: 2 Pr, 1 1/2 Br, 1 1/2 Ve 1/2 Sl, 1 OC
297 Calories, 6 gm Fa, 22 gm Pr, 38 gm Ca, 576 mg So
Diabetic: 2 Mt, 2 St, 1 Ve

CHICKEN—RICE—BROCCOLI BAKE

2 cups cooked rice
4 oz diced cooked chicken breast (scant 1 cup)
2 cups frozen cut broccoli, cooked and drained
1 oz sliced almonds (1/4 cup)
2/3 cup non fat dry milk powder
1 cup water
1 1/2 oz shredded reduced fat Cheddar cheese
    (1/3 cup)
1/8 teaspoon lemon pepper
2 Tablespoons reduced sodium soy sauce

Preheat oven to 350 degrees. In medium bowl combine rice, chicken, broccoli and almonds. In small bowl combine dry milk powder and water. Add cheese, lemon pepper and soy sauce. Mix well to combine. Pour cheese mixture over rice mixture. Stir well. Pour into an 8x8 baking dish sprayed with butter flavored cooking spray. Bake 30 minutes or until hot and cheese is melted through.

Serves 4
Each serving equals:
HE: 1 3/4 Pr, 1 Ve, 1 Br, 1/2 Fa, 1/2 SM
237 Calories, 6 gm Fa, 20 gm Pr, 25 gm Ca, 211 mg So
Diabetic: 2 Mt, 2 St, 1 Ve

TACO CHICKEN WITH VEGETABLES

1 cup frozen whole kernel corn, thawed
1 1/2 cups frozen green beans, thawed
1 1/2 cups frozen carrot slices, thawed
3/4 cup chopped onion
1 3/4 cups Mexican style stewed tomatoes, drained
1 (1.25 oz) pkg taco seasoning
16 oz boned and skinned chicken breasts
    cut into 4 serving pieces

Preheat oven to 350 degrees. In large bowl combine corn, beans, carrots and onions. Stir in drained stewed tomatoes and 2 Tablespoons taco seasoning mix. Pour into 8x8 baking dish sprayed with butter flavored cooking spray. Pat remaining taco seasoning onto all sides of chicken breasts. Place seasoned chicken on top of vegetables. Bake 35-45 minutes or until chicken is done. When serving, evenly spoon vegetables over chicken.

Serves 4
Each serving equals:
HE: 3 Pr, 2 3/4 Ve, 1/2 Br
228 Calories, 2 gm Fa, 30 gm Pr, 23 gm Ca, 412 mg So
Diabetic: 3 Mt, 2 Ve, 1/2 St

TURKEY WITH VEGETABLE SAUCE

1/2 cup chopped onion
1/4 cup chopped green bell pepper
1/2 teaspoon minced garlic
1/2 teaspoon dried thyme leaves
2 1/4 cups fresh tomato, seeded and coarsely chopped
1/2 teaspoon lemon pepper
2 teaspoons Sprinkle Sweet
12 oz baked sliced turkey breast

In large skillet sprayed with butter flavored cooking spray saute onion, green pepper and garlic until crisp-tender. Add thyme, tomatoes, lemon pepper and Sprinkle Sweet. Simmer uncovered for 5 minutes. Warm turkey slices in microwave. For each serving place 1/4 of turkey slices on plate. Spoon sauce evenly over turkey. Serve at once.

Serves 4
Each serving equals:
HE: 3 Pr, 1 1/2 Ve, 1 OC
147 Calories, 1 gm Fa, 27 gm Pr, 7 gm Ca, 191 mg So
Diabetic: 3 Mt, 1 Ve

PARTY TURKEY TETRAZZINI

1/2 cup chopped onion
8 oz diced cooked turkey breast (1 1/2 cups)
1 can Campbell's Healthy Request
    Cream of Mushroom soup
3 oz shredded reduced fat Cheddar cheese (3/4 cup)
2 cups cooked spaghetti, cut in pieces
2 Tablespoons chopped pimento
2 Tablespoons chopped fresh parsley
    or 1 teaspoon dried parsley flakes
1/8 teaspoon pepper

In large skillet sprayed with butter flavored cooking spray saute onion and turkey until onion is tender. Blend in soup and cheese. Cook over low heat until cheese is melted, stirring often. Add spaghetti, pimento, parsley and pepper. Continue cooking until heated through.

Serves 4
Each serving equals:
HE: 3 Pr, 1 Br, 1/4 Ve, 1/2 SL, 1 OC
271 Calories, 5 gm Fa, 27 gm Pr, 29 gm Ca, 516 mg So
Diabetic: 2 1/2 Mt, 2 St

HINT: Chicken or ham can be substituted for turkey.

TUNA POTATO CAKES

12 oz boiled potatoes, mashed (2 cups)
6 oz tuna, packed in water, drained and flaked
1 egg, beaten or equivalent in egg substitute
1 teaspoon Worcestershire sauce
1/4 cup chopped onion
1/4 cup finely chopped green bell pepper
2 teaspoons dried parsley flakes
1/2 teaspoon lemon pepper

In medium bowl combine potatoes, tuna, egg, Worcestershire sauce, onion, green pepper, parsley flakes and lemon pepper., Mix well. Form into 4 patties. Spray skillet with butter flavored cooking spray. Brown patties on both sides.

Serves 4
Each serving equals:
HE: 1 Pr (1/4 limited), 3/4 Br, 1/4 Ve
191 Calories, 2 gm Fa, 15 gm Pr, 29 gm Ca, 315 mg So
Diabetic: 2 Mt, 1 St

CHEESY TUNA NOODLE BAKE

3 cups cooked noodles
1 cup frozen peas
1 Tablespoon dried onion flakes
1 can Campbell's Healthy Request
    Cream of Mushroom soup
6 oz tuna, packed in water, drained and flaked
3 3/4 oz shredded reduced fat Cheddar cheese
    (scant 1 cup)
1 Tablespoon Dijon mustard
1/8 teaspoon pepper

Preheat oven to 350 degrees. In large bowl combine noodles, peas, onion flakes and soup. Add tuna, cheese, mustard and pepper. Pour into 8x8 baking dish sprayed with butter flavored cooking spray. Cover and bake 30 minutes. Uncover and bake additional 5 minutes.

Serves 6
Each serving equals:
HE: 1 1/3 Pr, 1 1/3 Br, 28 OC
231 Calories, 5 gm Fa, 18 gm Pr, 28 gm Ca, 540 mg So
Diabetic: 1 1/2 Mt, 1 1/2 St

CAJUN FISH

16 oz white fish (orange roughy, sole or flounder),
  broken into 8 pieces
1 1/2 oz dry bread crumbs (6 Tablespoons)
1/4 cup finely chopped onions
1 Tablespoon + 1 teaspoon reduced calorie
  margarine
1 3/4 cups Cajun style stewed tomatoes

Preheat oven to 350 degrees. Rinse fish in cold water. Pat dry. Spray an 8x8 baking dish with butter flavored cooking spray. Place fish in dish. Sprinkle bread crumbs and onions evenly over fish. Dot with margarine. Bake, uncovered for 20 minutes. Pour tomatoes over fish and continue to bake 20 minutes longer.

Serves 4
Each serving equals:
HE: 1 1/2 Pr, 1 Ve, 1/2 Br, 1/2 Fa
185 Calories, 3 gm Fa, 24 gm Pr, 15 gm Ca, 515 mg So
Diabetic: 3 Mt, 1/2 Ve, 1/2 St

STUFFED BAKED FISH

1/2 cup chopped onion
4 slices reduced calorie white bread, crumbled
    (40 calories per slice)
1 teaspoon dried basil leaves
1/8 teaspoon pepper
4 (2 oz) white fish fillets
2 teaspoons reduced calorie margarine
1/2 teaspoon paprika

Heat oven to 400 degrees. In large skillet sprayed with butter flavored cooking spray saute onions until tender. Add bread crumbs, basil and pepper. Mix well. Layer stuffing mixture evenly in 8x8 baking dish sprayed with butter flavored cooking spray. Place fillets on top of stuffing. Melt margarine and drizzle over fish. Sprinkle paprika on top. Bake 15-20 minutes or until fish flakes easily.

Serves 4
Each serving equals:
HE: 3/4 Pr, 1/2 Br, 1/4 Fa, 1/4 Ve
103 Calories, 1 gm Fa, 14 gm Pr, 9 gm Ca, 145 mg So
Diabetic: 1 1/2 Mt, 1/2 St

SALMON—VEGETABLE CASSEROLE

1 can Campbell's Healthy Request
   Cream of Mushroom soup
1 cup skim milk
4 oz uncooked instant rice (1 1/3 cups)
4 oz fat free cream cheese, softened
6 oz canned salmon, flaked and boned
2 cups canned green beans, drained
2 cups canned carrots, drained
1 Tablespoon dried onion flakes
2 Tablespoons chopped pimento
1 oz canned French fried onion rings (1/3 cup)

Preheat oven to 350 degrees. In medium saucepan combine soup and milk. Heat until warm. Add rice. Cover and let stand 5 minutes. Add cream cheese, salmon, green beans, carrots, dried onion flakes and pimento. Mix well to combine. Spray an 8x8 baking dish with butter flavored cooking spray. Pour mixture into dish. Bake covered 30 minutes. Top with onion rings and continue baking uncovered additional 10 minutes.

Serves 4
Each serving equals:
HE: 2 Ve, 2 Pr, 1 Br, 1/4 SM, 1/2 Sl, 9 OC
327 Calories, 7 gm Fa, 20 gm Pr, 46 gm Ca, 1013 mg So
Diabetic: 2 Ve, 2 Pr, 2 St

PORK CUTLETS WITH CORN STUFFING

4 (3 oz) lean pork cutlets or tenderloins
1/4 cup chopped onion
1/4 cup chopped green bell pepper
2 cups cream style corn
1 egg, beaten or equivalent in egg substitute
2 slices reduced calorie bread, crumbled
    (40 calories per slice)
1/8 teaspoon pepper

Preheat oven to 350 degrees. In large skillet sprayed with butter flavored cooking spray brown cutlets. Place browned cutlets in 8x8 baking dish. In medium bowl combine onion, green pepper, corn, egg, bread, and pepper. Mix well to combine. Place corn stuffing mixture on top of cutlets. Cover. Bake 1 hour.

Serves 4
Each serving equals:
HE: 2 1/2 Pr (1/4 limited), 1 1/4 Br, 1/4 Ve
278 Calories, 8 gm Fa, 24 gm Pr, 28 gm Ca, 466 mg So
Diabetic: 2 1/2 Mt, 2 St

HINT: Don't over brown cutlets or meat will turn
        out tough.

PORK CUTLETS CREOLE

4 (3 oz) lean pork cutlets or tenderloins
1/8 teaspoon pepper
4 slices onion
4 rings green bell pepper
1 3/4 cups Hunt's Chunky Tomato Sauce
1/8 teaspoon thyme
1/4 cup water
1 teaspoon Brown Sugar Twin
1/2 cup cooked rice

Preheat oven to 350 degrees. In skillet sprayed with butter flavored cooking spray brown cutlets. Place browned cutlets in 8 x 8 baking dish. Sprinkle each cutlet with pepper. Top each with onion slice and green pepper ring. In medium bowl combine tomato sauce, thyme, water, Brown Sugar Twin and cooked rice. Pour mixture over cutlets. Cover. Bake 30 minutes.

Serves 4
Each serving equals:
HE: 2 1/4 Pr, 2 Ve, 1/4 Br, 1 OC
247 Calories, 8 gm Fa, 21 gm Pr, 23 gm Ca, 647 mg So
Diabetic: 2 1/2 Mt, 2 Ve, 1/2 St

HINT: Don't over brown cutlets or meat will turn out tough.

YANKEE NOODLE BAKE

8 oz sliced Healthy Choice 97% fat free frankfurters
1/2 cup chopped green bell pepper
1/2 cup chopped onion
2 cups cooked noodles
1 3/4 cups Hunt's Chunky Tomato Sauce
1 Tablespoon Brown Sugar Twin
1 teaspoon prepared mustard
1/8 teaspoon pepper

Preheat oven to 350 degrees. In skillet sprayed with butter flavored cooking spray brown frankfurters, green pepper and onion. Add noodles, tomato sauce, Brown Sugar Twin, mustard and pepper. Mix well to combine. Pour into an 8x8 baking dish. Bake 30 minutes.

Serves 4
Each serving equals:
HE: 2 1/4 Ve, 1 1/3 Pr, 1 Br, 1 OC
226 Calories, 4 gm Fa, 13 gm Pr, 35 gm Ca, 1203 mg So
Diabetic: 2 Ve, 1 Mt, 1 St

POTATO AND SAUSAGE SALAD

16 oz cooked potatoes, cooled, peeled and sliced
   (3 cups)
2 Tablespoons cider vinegar
1/4 cup chopped onions or 4 chopped green onions
1/2 cup fat free mayonnaise
   (8 calories per Tablespoon)
2 teaspoons prepared horseradish
1/8 teaspoon pepper
1 teaspoon caraway seed
6 oz Healthy Choice 97% fat free Kielbasa sausage,
   cooked, cooled and sliced
3 oz shredded reduced fat Swiss cheese (3/4 cup)

Place sliced potatoes in large bowl. Gently mix in
vinegar and onions. In small bowl combine mayonnaise,
horseradish, pepper and caraway seed. Add to
potatoes. Stir in sausage and cheese. Mix gently to
combine. Chill until ready to serve.

Serves 6 (3/4 cup)
Each serving equals:
HE: 1 1/3 Pr, 2/3 Br, 13 OC
162 Calories, 4 gm Fa, 9 gm Pr, 23 gm Ca, 622 mg So
Diabetic: 1 Mt, 1 St

HINT: If you can't find Healthy Choice Kielbasa, use
      Healthy Choice frankfurters.

SAUSAGE AND SAUERKRAUT CASSEROLE

8 oz Healthy Choice 97% fat free Kielbasa sausage,
    cooked, cooled and sliced
2 cups cooked noodles
2 cups sauerkraut, well drained
1 can Campbell's Healthy Request
    Cream of Mushroom soup
1 teaspoon caraway seed
1/8 teaspoon pepper

Preheat oven to 350 degrees. In medium bowl combine sausage, noodles and sauerkraut. Add soup, caraway seed and pepper. Mix well to combine. Pour into 8x8 baking dish sprayed with cooking spray. Cover. Bake 45 minutes. Uncover and bake an additional 15 minutes.

Serves 4
Each serving equals:
HE: 1 1/3 Pr, 1 Br, 1 Ve, 1/2 Sl, 4 OC
247 Calories, 5 gm Fa, 16 gm Pr, 35 gm Ca, 1562 mg So
Diabetic: 1 1/2 Mt, 1 1/2 St, 1 Ve

HINT: If you can't find Healthy Choice Kielbasa, use
    Healthy Choice frankfurters.

RED FLANNEL HASH

1/2 cup finely chopped onion

10 oz frozen shredded potatoes, thawed (3 full cups)

2 cups canned beets,
    drained and finely chopped

5 oz finely chopped corned beef (90% lean)

1/8 teaspoon pepper

1/3 cup non fat dry milk powder

1/2 cup water

1 Tablespoon + 1 teaspoon reduced
    calorie margarine

In large skillet sprayed with butter flavored cooking spray saute onions until tender. Place onions in large bowl. Add potatoes, beets, corned beef and pepper. In small bowl combine dry milk powder and water. Add to potato mixture. Mix gently until well blended. Melt margarine in same skillet. Evenly spread hash mixture in skillet. Cook over medium heat until browned.

Serves 4
Each serving equals:
HE: 1 1/4 Pr, 1 1/4 Ve, 1/2 Br, 1/2 Fa 1/4 SM
175 Calories, 4 gm Fa, 11 gm Pr, 24 gm Ca, 792 mg So
Diabetic: 1 Mt, 1 Ve, 1 St

HINT: 1) Carl Buddig corned beef works great.
       2) Mr. Dell's shredded potatoes work great

REUBEN CASSEROLE

1/4 cup fat free Thousand Island dressing
    (20 calories per Tablespoon)
1/4 cup fat free mayonnaise
    (8 calories per Tablespoon)
2 cups sauerkraut, drained
3 oz sliced corned beef (90% lean)
3 oz shredded reduced fat Swiss cheese (3/4 cup)
1 cup sliced fresh tomato
2 slices reduced calorie Rye bread
    cut into small pieces (40 calories per slice)

Preheat oven to 350 degrees. In small bowl combine mayonnaise and Thousand Island dressing. Layering in an 8x8 baking dish, place sauerkraut on bottom, then corned beef, dressing mixture, cheese and tomatoes. In a non-stick pan, sprayed with butter flavored cooking spray, lightly toast bread. Sprinkle on top of tomatoes. Bake 20 minutes.

Serves 4
Each serving equals:
HE: 1 3/4 Pr, 1 1/2 Ve, 1/4 Br, 28 OC
189 Calories, 7 gm Fa, 11 gm Pr, 21 gm Ca, 1663 mg So
Diabetic: 1 1/2 Mt, 1 Ve, 1 St

HINT: Carl Buddig Corned Beef works great.

ST. PADDY'S POTATO CASSEROLE

1 cup diced onion
10 oz frozen shredded potatoes, thawed (3 full cups)
3 cups shredded cabbage
2 cups sliced canned carrots, drained
5 oz diced corned beef <u>or</u> ham (90% lean)
3 oz shredded reduced fat Swiss cheese (3/4 cup)
1 can Campbell's Special Request
    Cream of Mushroom soup
1/8 teaspoon pepper

Preheat oven to 350 degrees. In large skillet sprayed with cooking spray brown onions. Add potatoes, cabbage, carrots, meat, 1/2 cup Swiss cheese, soup, and pepper. Mix well to combine. Pour into an 8x8 baking dish sprayed with butter flavored cooking spray. Bake 45 minutes. Top with remaining cheese. Bake another 10 minutes. Let cool 10 minutes before serving.

Serves 4
Each serving equals:
HE: 3 Ve, 2 1/4 Pr, 1/2 Br, 1/2 Sl, 1 OC
264 Calories, 9 gm Fa, 15 gm Pr, 31 gm Ca, 1337 mg So
Diabetic: 2 Ve, 2 Mt, 1 St

HINT: 1) Carl Buddig Corned beef works great.
      2) Mr. Dell's shredded potatoes work great.

CABBAGE—HAM QUICHE

1 purchased unbaked refrigerated 9" pie crust
6 oz diced Dubuque 97% fat free ham (full 1 cup)
1/2 cup chopped onion
3 1/2 cups chopped cabbage
1 cup hot water
2/3 cup non fat dry milk powder
1 cup cold water
2 eggs, slightly beaten or equivalent in egg substitute
3 oz shredded reduced fat Swiss cheese (3/4 cup)
1/8 teaspoon pepper
1/2 teaspoon caraway seed

Bake pie crust according to package directions until almost done. Remove from oven. Lower heat to 375 degrees. Saute ham and onion in skillet sprayed with butter flavored cooking spray until onion is tender. Add cabbage and water. Continue cooking until liquid evaporates and cabbage is golden brown, about 12 minutes. Remove from heat. In small bowl combine dry milk powder, cold water, eggs, cheese, pepper and caraway seed. Stir into cabbage mixture. Pour into partially baked crust. Bake until filling puffs and starts to brown about 40 minutes.

Serves 8
Each serving equals:
HE: 1 1/4 Pr (1/4 limited), 1 Ve, 1/2 Br, 1/4 SM, 1/2 Sl, 10 OC
233 Calories, 12 gm Fa, 11 gm Pr, 20 gm Ca, 538 mg So
Diabetic: 1 Mt, 1 Ve, 1 St, 1 Fa

HAM AND GREEN BEAN CASSEROLE

1 can Campbell's Healthy Request
   Cream of Mushroom soup
4 cups canned green beans, drained
6 oz diced Dubuque 97% fat free ham (full 1 cup)
1/8 teaspoon pepper
3 oz shredded reduced fat Cheddar cheese (3/4 cup)

In large bowl combine soup, beans, ham and pepper. Pour into an 8x8 baking dish sprayed with butter flavored cooking spray. Microwave for 6 minutes on high or until hot. Sprinkle cheese over top. Microwave 2 minutes more or until cheese melts.

Serves 4
Each serving equals:
HE: 2 Pr, 2 Ve, 1/2 Sl, 1 OC
168 Calories, 6 gm Fa, 15 gm Pr, 14 gm Ca, 1179 mg So
Diabetic: 2 Mt, 2 Ve

HAWAIIAN BRUNCH CASSEROLE

1 cup canned crushed pineapple, packed in its
    own juice, drained, reserve liquid
3/4 cup Bisquick reduced fat baking mix
2/3 cup nonfat dry milk powder
2 eggs, slightly beaten or equivalent in egg substitute
2 teaspoons reduced calorie margarine, melted
1 teaspoon Dijon mustard
1/2 teaspoon onion powder or dried onion flakes
3 oz diced Dubuque 97% fat free ham (1/2 cup)
3 oz shredded reduced fat Cheddar cheese (3/4 cup)
1 finely chopped green onion

Preheat oven to 350 degrees. Add enough water to reserved pineapple juice to make 3/4 cup liquid. Combine pineapple liquid, baking mix, dry milk powder, eggs, margarine, mustard and onion powder in blender. Process on blend 45 seconds. Pour into medium bowl. Stir in ham, cheese, onion and pineapple. Pour into 8x8 baking dish sprayed with butter flavored cooking spray. Bake 25-30 minutes.

Serves 4
Each serving equals:
HE: 2 Pr (1/2 limited), 1 Br, 1/2 SM, 1/2 Fr, 1/4 Fa
283 Calories, 9 gm Fa, 19 gm Pr, 32 gm Ca, 727 mg So
Diabetic: 2 Mt, 1 St, 1/2 SM, 1/2 Fr

HAM ROTINI

2 cups cooked Rotini noodles
2 cups canned sliced carrots, drained
2 cups canned green beans, drained
6 oz diced Dubuque 97% fat free ham (full 1 cup)
2/3 cup non fat dry milk powder
1 cup water
3 oz shredded reduced fat Cheddar cheese (3/4 cup)
1/4 teaspoon lemon pepper

Preheat oven to 350 degrees. In medium bowl combine noodles, carrots, green beans and ham. Place in 8x8 baking dish sprayed with butter flavored cooking spray. In small bowl combine dry milk powder, water, cheese and lemon pepper. Pour milk mixture over noodle mixture. Bake 30 minutes or until hot and cheese is melted.

Serves 4
Each serving equals:
HE: 2 Pr, 2 Ve, 1 Br, 1/2 SM
284 Calories, 6 gm Fa, 22 gm Pr, 35 gm Ca, 948 mg So
Diabetic: 2 Mt, 2 Ve, 1 St, 1/2 SM

DESSERTS

K.P. MILLER
8/91

DESSERTS

BAKED APPLES

4 small Rome Beauty apples
4 Tablespoons raisins
1 oz chopped walnuts (1/4 cup)
1 Tablespoon + 1 teaspoon reduced
   calorie margarine, melted
1 Tablespoon Brown Sugar Twin
1/4 cup lemon juice
1/4 cup water
1 teaspoon apple pie spice

Preheat oven to 350 degrees. Pare apple skin 1/3 way down from top of apple. Core and splice apples, leaving bottom attached. Place apples in 8x8 baking dish. In small bowl combine raisins, walnuts, margarine and Brown Sugar Twin. Stuff mixture in the center of the apples. In small bowl combine lemon juice, water and apple pie spice. Pour over and around apples. Bake, uncovered 30-40 minutes or until apples are tender. Baste every 10 minutes.

Serves 4
Each serving equals:
HE: 1 1/2 Fr, 1 Fa, 1/4 Pr, 2 OC
141 Calories, 6 gm Fa, 1 gm Pr, 21 gm Ca, 23 mg So
Diabetic: 1 1/2 Fr, 1 Fa

BLACK FOREST PIE

1 purchased 9" chocolate crumb pie crust
1 1/2 cups cold water
1 (4 serving) pkg sugar free cherry gelatin
1 (4 serving) pkg sugar free vanilla cook and
        serve pudding mix
2 cups pitted red cherries,
    fresh or canned - packed in water, drained
1/2 teaspoon almond extract

In medium saucepan combine water, dry gelatin, dry pudding mix and cherries. Bring mixture to a boil. Continue to cook about 2 minutes, stirring constantly. Remove from heat; add almond extract. Let set about 5 minutes. Pour into chocolate crumb pie crust. Chill about 2 hours.

TOPPING:
1 (8 oz) pkg fat free cream cheese
1/4 cup reduced calorie whipped topping
    (8 calories per Tablespoon)
1 teaspoon vanilla extract
Sugar substitute to equal 2 teaspoons sugar

In medium bowl stir cream cheese with a spoon until soft. Add whipped topping, vanilla extract and sugar substitute. Spread mixture evenly over set pie. Sprinkle 1 oz (1/4 cup) chopped walnuts evenly over top. Chill until ready to serve.

Serves 8
Each serving equals:
HE: 2/3 Pr, 1/2 Fr, 1/2 Br, 1/4 Fa, 1/2 Sl, 28 OC
201 Calories, 7 gm Fa, 7 gm Pr, 27 gm Ca, 372 mg So
Diabetic: 1 Fr, 1 St, 1 Fa

CHERRIES JUBILEE PIE

1 purchased 9" butter flavored pie crust
1 (4 serving) pkg sugar free instant
   vanilla pudding mix
2/3 cup nonfat dry milk powder
1 1/4 cups water
1 cup reduced calorie whipped topping
   (8 calories per Tablespoon)
1/2 teaspoon Brandy extract
12 oz pitted bing cherries (2 cups)

In medium bowl combine dry pudding mix and dry milk powder. Add water. Mix well to combine, using a wire whisk. Blend in 1/2 cup whipped topping and Brandy extract. Fold in cherries. Pour into pie crust. Chill until set about 2 hours. Spread remaining 1/2 cup whipped topping evenly over top. Continue chilling until ready to serve.

Serves 8
Each serving equals:
HE: 1/2 Br, 1/2 Fr. 1/4 SM, 1/2 Sl, 39 OC
189 Calories, 6 gm Fa, 3 gm Pr, 31 gm Ca, 316 mg So
Diabetic: 1 St, 1 Fr, 1 Fa

FRESH PEACH PIE

1 purchased 9" butter flavored or
    graham cracker pie crust
4 medium peaches, peeled and sliced
1 (4 serving) pkg sugar free lemon gelatin
1 (4 serving) pkg sugar free vanilla
    cook and serve pudding mix
1 1/2 cups water
1/2 cup reduced calorie whipped topping
    (8 calories per Tablespoon)
Dash nutmeg

Layer peaches in pie crust. In medium saucepan combine dry gelatin, dry pudding mix and water. Bring mixture to a boil, stirring constantly. Pour hot mixture over peaches.Cool until set, about 2 hours. When serving, top each slice with 1 Tablespoon whipped topping. Sprinkle with a dash of nutmeg.

Serves 8
Each serving equals:
HE: 1/2 Br, 1/2 Fr, 1/2 Sl, 32 OC
151 Calories, 5 gm Fa, 2 gm Pr, 24 gm Ca, 222 mg So
Diabetic: 1 St, 1 Fa, 1/2 Fr

PEACH PRALINE PIE

1 purchased 9" unbaked refrigerated pie crust
1/4 cup Cary's reduced calorie maple syrup
   (10 calories per tablespoon)
4 Tablespoons Brown Sugar Twin
4 cups canned peaches, packed in fruit juice, drained
3 Tablespoons instant tapioca
1 oz chopped pecans (1/4 cup)

Place pie crust in 9" pie plate. Flute edges. Preheat oven to 425 degrees. In large bowl combine maple syrup and Brown Sugar Twin. Blend in peaches. Mix in tapioca. Let mixture set 5 minutes. Blend in pecans. Pour mixture into pie crust. Bake 35-40 minutes or until crust is golden brown. Remove from oven and place on cooling rack. Cool at least 2 hours before serving. Good topped with 1 Tablespoon reduced calorie whipped topping. If using, count optional calories accordingly.

Serves 8
Each serving equals:
HE: 1 Fr, 1/2 Br, 1/2 Fa, 1/2 Sl, 30 OC
225 Calories, 10 gm Fa, 2 gm Pr, 32 gm Ca, 154 mg So
Diabetic: 2 Fa, 1 Fr, 1 St

FRUIT COCKTAIL CHIFFON PIE

1 purchased 9" graham cracker pie crust
1 (8 oz) pkg fat free cream cheese
1 (4 serving) pkg sugar free instant
    vanilla pudding mix
2/3 cup nonfat dry milk powder
1 cup water
1 cup reduced calorie whipped topping
    (8 calories per Tablespoon)
2 cups canned fruit cocktail, packed
    in its own juice, drained

In large mixing bowl stir cream cheese with spoon until soft. Add dry pudding mix, dry milk powder and water. Mix well using a wire whisk. Fold in 1/2 cup whipped topping. Add fruit cocktail. Mix gently to combine. Pour into pie crust. Chill at least 4 hours. When serving, top each piece with 1 Tablespoon reduced calorie whipped topping.

Serves 8
Each serving equals:
HE: 1/2 Br, 1/2 Fr, 1/2 Pr, 1/4 SM, 1/2 Sl, 39 OC
221 Calories, 7 gm Fa, 8 gm Pr, 31 gm Ca, 439 mg So
Diabetic: 1 St, 1 Fr, 1 Fa

PINEAPPLE FLUFF PIE

1 purchased 9" graham cracker pie crust
1 (4 serving) pkg sugar free instant
    vanilla pudding mix
2/3 cup nonfat dry milk powder
1 cup water
1 cup canned crushed pineapple, packed in
    its own juice, drained
1 (4 serving) pkg sugar free Hawaiian
    pineapple gelatin
1 (8 oz) pkg fat free cream cheese
1 cup reduced calorie whipped topping
    (8 calories per Tablespoon)
3-4 drops yellow food coloring

In large bowl combine dry pudding mix, dry milk powder, water and drained pineapple. Mix well using a wire whisk. Blend in dry gelatin. In medium bowl stir cream cheese with spoon until soft. Blend in whipped topping and food coloring.Add to pudding mixture. Mix gently to combine. Pour into pie crust. Chill.

Serves 8
Each serving equals:
HE: 1/2 Pr, 1/2 Br, 1/4 Fr, 1/4 SM, 1 Sl, 3 OC
221 Calories, 7 gm Fa, 8 gm Pr, 31 gm Ca, 544 mg So
Diabetic: 1 St, 1 Fr, 1 Fa

RHUBARB FLUFF PIE

1 purchased 9" graham cracker pie crust
4 cups rhubarb (cut into 1" pieces)
1 cup water
1 (4 serving) pkg sugar free strawberry gelatin
1 (4 serving) pkg sugar free vanilla cook and serve
    pudding mix
1 1/2 cups reduced calorie whipped topping
    (8 calories per Tablespoon)

In medium saucepan combine rhubarb, water, dry
gelatin and dry pudding mix. Bring mixture to a boil,
stirring often. Simmer until rhubarb is soft. Remove
from heat. Let cool until almost set; then whip until
thick with electric mixer. Fold in whipped topping. Pour
mixture into pie crust. Chill several hours before
serving.

Serves 8
Each serving equals:
HE: 1 Ve, 1/2 Br, 1 Sl, 8 OC
171 Calories, 7 gm Fa, 2 gm Pr, 25 gm Ca, 250 mg So
Diabetic: 1 1/2 St, 1 Fa

CHOCOLATE PEANUT BUTTER PIE

1 purchased 9" butter flavored pie crust
3 Tablespoons peanut butter, creamy or chunky
1 (4 serving) pkg sugar free instant
    chocolate pudding mix
2 cups skim milk
1/2 cup reduced calorie whipped topping
    (8 calories per Tablespoon)
1/2 oz chopped dry roasted peanuts (2 Tablespoons)

Soften peanut butter to room temperature. In medium bowl combine dry pudding mix and milk. Mix well using a wire whisk. Blend in softened peanut butter. Pour pudding mixture into pie crust. Chill 30 minutes. Evenly spread whipped topping over set pie filling. Garnish top with chopped peanuts. Chill until ready to serve.

Serves 8
Each serving equals:
HE: 1/2 Fa, 1/3 Pr, 1/2 Br, 1/4 SM, 1/2 Sl, 34 OC
209 Calories, 10 gm Fa, 5 gm Pr, 25 gm Ca, 346 mg So
Diabetic: 1 1/2 Fa, 1 St, 1/2 SM

CHOCO MINT PIE

1 purchased 9" chocolate crumb pie crust
1 (4 serving) pkg sugar free instant
    vanilla pudding mix
2/3 cup nonfat dry milk powder
1 1/4 cups water
1/2 teaspoon mint extract
2-3 drops green food coloring
1 cup reduced calorie whipped topping
    (8 calories per Tablespoon)
1/2 oz mini chocolate chips (2 Tablespoons)

In medium bowl combine dry pudding mix, dry milk powder and water. Mix well using a wire whisk. Fold in mint extract, green food coloring and whipped topping. Stir in chocolate chips. Pour into pie crust. Chill at least 4 hours before serving.

Serves 8
Each serving equals:
HE: 1/2 Br, 1/4 SM, 1 Sl, 7 OC
169 Calories, 6 gm Fa, 3 gm Pr, 25 gm Ca, 291 mg So
Diabetic: 1 1/2 St, 1 Fa

ROCKY ROAD PIE

1 purchased 9" butter flavored pie crust
1 (8 oz) pkg fat free cream cheese
1 cup reduced calorie whipped topping
    (8 calories per Tablespoon)
1 teaspoon vanilla extract
1 (4 serving) pkg sugar free instant
    chocolate pudding mix
2/3 cup nonfat dry milk powder
1 1/3 cups water
1/2 oz mini chocolate chips (2 Tablespoons)
1/2 oz chopped pecans (2 Tablespoons)

In medium bowl stir cream cheese with spoon until soft. Blend in 1/2 cup whipped topping and vanilla extract. Spread in bottom of pie crust. In medium bowl combine dry pudding mix, dry milk powder and water. Mix well using a wire whisk. Pour over cream cheese layer. Chill 2 hours. Spread remaining 1/2 cup whipped topping over set pudding mixture. Sprinkle top with chocolate chips and pecans.

Serves 8
Each serving equals:
HE: 1/2 Pr, 1/2 Br, 1/4 SM, 1/4 Fa, 1 Sl, 8 OC
211 Calories, 8 gm Fa, 8 gm Pr, 27 gm Ca, 486 mg So
Diabetic: 2 St, 1 Fa

PISTACHIO CREAM PIE

1 purchased 9" butter flavored pie crust
1 (4 serving) pkg sugar free instant
    pistachio pudding mix
2/3 cup nonfat dry milk powder
1 1/3 cups water
1 cup canned crushed pineapple, packed in
    its own juice, drained
1 cup reduced calorie whipped topping
    (8 calories per Tablespoon)

In large bowl combine dry pudding mix, dry milk powder and water. Mix well using a wire whisk. Blend in crushed pineapple and whipped topping. Mix well to combine. Pour into pie crust. Chill 3-4 hours before serving.

Serves 8
Each serving equals:
HE: 1/2 Br, 1/4 SM, 1/4 Fr, 1/2 Sl, 39 OC
180 Calories, 6 gm Fa, 3 gm Pr, 29 gm Ca, 321 mg So
Diabetic: 1 St, 1 Fr, 1 Fa

PUMPKIN CHIFFON PIE

1 purchased 9" graham cracker pie crust
2 cups canned pumpkin
1 (4 serving) pkg sugar free instant
    vanilla pudding mix
2/3 cup nonfat dry milk powder
1 teaspoon pumpkin pie spice
3/4 cup water
1 cup reduced calorie whipped topping
    (8 calories per Tablespoon)
1/2 oz chopped pecans (2 Tablespoons)

In medium bowl combine pumpkin, dry pudding mix, dry milk powder, pumpkin pie spice and water. Mix well using a wire whisk. Blend in 1/4 cup whipped topping. Pour mixture into pie crust. Chill 2 hours. Spread remaining 3/4 cup whipped topping over top of set filling. Sprinkle pecans evenly on top.

Serves 8
Each serving equals:
HE: 1/2 Br, 1/2 Ve, 1/4 SM, 1/4 Fa, 1/2 Sl, 39 OC
206 Calories, 8 gm Fa, 4 gm Pr, 30 gm Ca, 350 mg So
Diabetic: 2 St, 1 Fa

BUTTERSCOTCH-RAISIN MERINGUE PIE

1 purchased 9" unbaked refrigerated pie crust
1 (4 serving) pkg sugar free vanilla cook and
    serve pudding mix
2 cups skim milk
1 (4 serving) pkg sugar free instant
    butterscotch pudding mix
1/2 cup raisins
6 egg whites
Sugar substitute to equal 6 Tablespoons sugar
1 teaspoon vanilla extract

Bake pie shell according to package directions. Cool. In medium saucepan combine dry vanilla pudding mix and skim milk. Cook over medium heat, stirring constantly, until mixture comes to a boil. Remove from heat. Cool 10 minutes. Stir in dry instant butterscotch pudding mix and raisins. Pour into cooled pie crust. In medium bowl whip egg whites with electric mixer until fluffy. Add sugar substitute and vanilla. Continue whipping until soft peaks form. Spread evenly over filling, being sure to completely seal to edges of pie crust. Bake at 425 degrees for 6-7 minutes or until meringue starts to brown. Cool on wire rack.

Serves 8
Each serving equals:
HE: 1/2 Br, 1/2 Fr, 1/4 SM, 1/4 Pr, 1/2 Sl, 37 OC
208 Calories, 7 gm Fa, 6 gm Pr, 30 gm Ca, 446 mg So
Diabetic: 1 Fr, 1 Fa, 1 St

HINT: I)   Eggs beat best at room temperature.
       2)   Meringue pie cuts easily if you dip sharp
           knife in warm water before slicing.

CHERRY CRUNCH

3 oz quick oats (1 cup)
6 Tablespoons flour
3 Tablespoons Brown Sugar Twin
1/4 cup reduced calorie margarine, melted
3 cups cherries, pitted or canned,
    packed in water, drained
1 1/2 cups water
1 (4 serving) pkg sugar free cherry gelatin
1 (4 serving) pkg sugar free cook and serve
    vanilla pudding mix
1/4 teaspoon almond extract

Preheat oven to 350 degrees. In medium bowl, combine oats, flour and Brown Sugar Twin until well blended. Add melted margarine. Mix until crumbly. Spray an 8x8 baking dish with butter flavored cooking spray. Spread half of the crumb mixture on bottom of pan. Place drained cherries on top of crumbs. In medium saucepan combine water, dry gelatin and dry pudding mix. Cook to boiling, stirring constantly. Remove from heat. Stir in almond extract. Pour hot mixture over cherries. Top with remaining crumbs. Bake 45 minutes. Cool over wire rack.

Serves 6
Each serving equals:
HE: 1 Fr, 1 Br, 1 Fa, 21 OC
171 Calories, 3 gm Fa, 5 gm Pr, 31 gm Ca, 175 mg So
Diabetic: 1 Fr, 1 St, 1/2 Fa

HINT: Good served with 1 Tablespoon reduced calorie
        whipped topping. If using, count additional
        calories accordingly.

RHUBARB CRUNCH

3 oz quick oats (1 cup)
6 Tablespoons flour
1 teaspoon cinnamon
3 Tablespoons Brown Sugar Twin
1/4 cup reduced calorie margarine, melted
4 cups diced rhubarb
1 (4 serving) pkg sugar free strawberry gelatin
1 (4 serving) pkg sugar free cook and serve
    vanilla pudding mix
1 1/2 cups water
1 teaspoon vanilla extract

Preheat oven to 350 degrees. In medium bowl combine oats, flour, cinnamon and Brown Sugar Twin until well blended. Add melted margarine. Mix until crumbly. Set aside. Place rhubarb in 8x8 baking dish. In medium saucepan combine dry gelatin, dry pudding mix and water. Cook to boiling, stirring constantly. Remove from heat. Stir in vanilla extract. Pour hot mixture over diced rhubarb. Top with crumbs. Bake 1 hour. Cool on a wire rack.

Serves 6
Each serving equals:
HE: 1 1/3 Ve, 1 Br, 1 Fa, 22 OC
142 Calories, 3 gm Fa, 5 gm Pr, 23 gm Ca, 170 mg So
Diabetic: 1 St, 1 Fa, 1 Free Food

HINT: Good served with 1 Tablespoon reduced calorie
        whipped topping. If using, count additional
        calories accordingly.

CARROT CAKE

2 Tablespoons vegetable oil
1 cup unsweetened applesauce
3 Tablespoons Brown Sugar Twin
3 Tablespoons Sprinkle Sweet
2 eggs, well beaten or equivalent in egg substitute
1 cup canned carrots, drained and diced
1/4 cup water
1 1/2 cups cake flour
1/2 teaspoon salt
1/2 teaspoon baking powder
1/2 teaspoon baking soda
1/2 teaspoon cinnamon
1 teaspoon vanilla extract
1/2 oz chopped walnuts (2 Tablespoons)
1/4 cup raisins

Preheat oven to 350 degrees. In large bowl combine oil, applesauce, Brown Sugar Twin and Sprinkle Sweet. Add eggs, carrots and water. Mix just to combine.In medium bowl combine flour, salt, baking powder, baking soda and cinnamon. Stir into carrot mixture. Add vanilla extract, walnuts and raisins. Mix gently to combine. Pour batter into an 8x8 baking dish sprayed with butter flavored cooking spray. Bake 30 minutes or until cake tests done. Cool on wire rack. Spread topping over top of cooled cake and garnish with walnuts.

Topping:
1 (8 oz pkg) fat free cream cheese
Sugar substitute to equal 2 teaspoons sugar
1/2 cup reduced calorie whipped topping
    (8 calories per tablespoon)
1 teaspoon vanilla extract
1/2 oz chopped walnuts (2 Tablespoons)

In medium bowl stir cream cheese with spoon until soft. Add sugar substitute, whipped topping and vanilla extract.

Serves 8
Each serving equals:
HE: 1 Fa, 1 Br, 3/4 Pr (1/4 limited), 1/2 Fr,1/4 Ve, 20 OC
215 Calories, 10 gm Fa, 7 gm Pr, 24 gm Ca, 504 mg So
Diabetic: 2 Fa, 1 St, 1 Fr

PINEAPPLE CAKE

2 Tablespoons vegetable oil
1/2 cup unsweetened applesauce
3 Tablespoons Brown Sugar Twin
3 Tablespoons Sprinkle Sweet
2 eggs, beaten or equivalent in egg substitute
2 Tablespoons raisins
2 cups canned crushed pineapple, packed
    in its own juice, drained (reserve liquid)
1 1/2 cups cake flour
1/2 teaspoon salt
1/2 teaspoon baking powder
1/2 teaspoon baking soda
1 teaspoon vanilla extract

Preheat oven to 350 degrees. In large bowl combine oil, applesauce, Brown Sugar Twin and Sprinkle Sweet. Add eggs, raisins and crushed pineapple. Add enough water to reserved pineapple juice to make 1/2 cup liquid. Add liquid to applesauce mixture. Mix just to combine. In medium bowl combine flour, salt, baking powder and baking soda. Stir into pineapple mixture. Add vanilla extract. Mix to combine. Pour batter into an 8x8 baking dish sprayed with butter flavored cooking spray. Bake 30 minutes or until cake tests done. Cool on wire rack.

Serves 8
Each serving equals:
HE: 1 Br, 3/4 Fa, 3/4 Fr, 1/4 Pr (limited), 5 OC
177 Calories, 7 gm Fa, 3 gm Pr, 26 gm Ca, 290 mg So
Diabetic: 1 St, 1 Fa, 1 Fr

HINT: Good served with 1 Tablespoon reduced calorie whipped topping. If using, count additional calories accordingly.

PUMPKIN CAKE

2 Tablespoons + 2 teaspoons vegetable oil
1/2 cup unsweetened applesauce
3 Tablespoons Brown Sugar Twin
3 Tablespoons Sprinkle Sweet
2 eggs, well beaten or equivalent in egg substitute
1 cup canned pumpkin
1/2 cup low fat buttermilk
1 1/2 cups cake flour
1/2 teaspoon salt
1/2 teaspoon baking powder
1/2 teaspoon baking soda
1/2 teaspoon cinnamon
1 teaspoon vanilla extract
1/2 cup + 2 Tablespoons raisins

Preheat oven to 350 degrees. In large bowl combine oil, applesauce, Brown Sugar Twin and Sprinkle Sweet. Add eggs and pumpkin. Mix well. Blend in buttermilk. In medium bowl combine flour, salt, baking powder, baking soda and cinnamon. Stir into pumpkin mixture. Add vanilla extract and raisins. Mix gently to combine. Pour batter into an 8x8 baking dish sprayed with butter flavored cooking spray. Bake 25-30 minutes or until cake tests done. Cool on wire rack.

Serves 8
Each serving equals:
HE: 1 Fa, 1 Br, 3/4 Fr, 1/4 Pr (limited), 1/4 Ve, 11 OC
205 Calories, 8 gm Fa, 4 gm Pr, 30 gm Ca, 294 mg So
Diabetic: 1 Fa, 1 St, 1 Fr

HINT: Good served with 1 Tablespoon reduced calorie whipped topping. If using, count additional calories accordingly.

STRAWBERRY TAPIOCA PUDDING

1 (4 serving) pkg sugar free strawberry gelatin
2 cups water
3 Tablespoons instant tapioca
2 cups frozen (no sugar added) strawberries, sliced
3/4 cup plain fat free yogurt
1/3 cup nonfat dry milk powder
1 cup reduced calorie whipped topping
    (8 calories per Tablespoon)
Sugar substitute to equal 4 teaspoons sugar

In medium saucepan combine dry gelatin, water and tapioca. Let set 5 minutes. Cook over medium heat. Bring mixture to a boil, stirring often. Remove from heat. Add frozen strawberries. Cool completely. In small bowl combine yogurt and dry milk powder. Blend in whipped topping and sugar substitute. Add to tapioca mixture. Mix well to combine. Spoon into 6 dessert dishes. Chill until ready to serve.

Serves 6 (3/4 cup)
Each serving equals:
HE: 1/3 Fr, 1/3 SM, 1/2 Sl, 3 OC
86 Calories, 1 gm Fa, 4 gm Pr, 15 gm Ca, 81 mg So
Diabetic: 1 St

CINNAMON PEACH BREAD PUDDING

8 slices reduced calorie bread
   (40 calories per slice)
1 Tablespoon + 1 teaspoon reduced
   calorie margarine
2 Tablespoons spreadable fruit peach spread
1 1/3 cups skim milk
2 eggs or equivalent in egg substitute
2 Tablespoons Sprinkle Sweet
1/2 teaspoon cinnamon
1 teaspoon vanilla extract
2 Tablespoons raisins

Toast bread. Spread with margarine and peach spreadable fruit. Cube bread. Pour milk into 4 cup glass measure. Scald, but do not boil milk in microwave about 4 to 7 minutes on high. Let cool. In large bowl stir eggs with wire whisk. Add Sprinkle Sweet, cinnamon and vanilla extract. Stir in scalded milk. Mix well to combine. Add bread and raisins. Mix well. Let set about 10 minutes for bread to absorb milk. Pour into 8 x 8 baking dish. Bake at 50% or medium power in microwave for about 10 minutes. Spoon into 4 dessert dishes.

Serves 4
Each serving equals:
HE: 1 Br, 3/4 Fr, 1/2 Fa, 1/2 Pr (limited),1/3 SM, 2 OC
197 Calories, 4 gm Fa, 12 gm Pr, 29 gm Ca, 280 mg So
Diabetic: 1 St, 1 Mt, 1 Fr

HINT: Good served warm with 1 Tablespoon reduced
      calorie whipped topping. If using, count optional
      calories accordingly.

FRUIT PIZZA

1 (8 serving) can Crescent refrigerated rolls
1 (8 oz) pkg fat free cream cheese
1 teaspoon vanilla extract
Sugar substitute to equal 2 teaspoons sugar
2 cups canned crushed pineapple, packed in
    its own juice, drained
2 cups fresh strawberries, sliced
1 1/2 cups blueberries, fresh or frozen,
    thawed and drained
1 (4 serving) pkg sugar free mixed fruit gelatin
1 (4 serving) pkg sugar free vanilla
    cook and serve pudding mix
1 1/2 cups water

Preheat oven to 425 degrees. Spray medium size pizza pan or cookie sheet with butter flavored cooking spray. Pat rolls in pan, being sure to seal perforations. Bake 7-8 minutes or until lightly browned. Cool on wire rack. In medium bowl stir cream cheese with spoon until soft. Blend in vanilla extract and sugar substitute. Spread mixture evenly over cooled crust. Layer pineapple over cream cheese mixture. Sprinkle strawberries and blueberries over pineapple. In medium saucepan combine dry gelatin, dry pudding mix and water. Cook over medium heat until mixture comes to a boil, stirring constantly. Spoon hot mixture evenly over fruit until entire pan is covered with glaze. Cool at least 2 hours before serving.

Serves 8
Each serving equals:
HE: 1 Br, 1 Fr, 1/2 Pr, 15 OC
204 Calories, 6 gm Fa, 7 gm Pr, 31 gm Ca, 501 mg So
Diabetic: 1 St, 1 Fr, 1 Fa

HINT: Do not use inexpensive rolls. They do not cover
    the pan properly.

HAWAIIAN FRUIT SQUARES

1 (8 serving) can Crescent refrigerated rolls
1 (8 oz) pkg fat free cream cheese
2 Tablespoons Sprinkle Sweet
1 Tablespoon lemon juice
1 teaspoon coconut extract
2 eggs or equivalent in egg substitute
3 Tablespoons flaked coconut
1 cup canned crushed pineapple, packed in its
   own juice, drained

Preheat oven to 375 degrees. Spray a 9 x 13 rimmed cookie sheet with butter flavored cooking spray. Pat rolls in pan being sure to seal perforations. Bake 5 minutes. Remove from oven. In medium bowl stir cream cheese with a spoon until soft. Add Sprinkle Sweet, lemon juice, coconut extract and eggs. Blend until smooth. Stir in coconut and pineapple. Mix well. Evenly spread mixture over partially baked crust. Bake an additional 20-25 minutes or until crust is golden brown and filling set. Cool completely on wire rack. Cut into 8 squares or 32 bars.

Serves 8 (1 square or 4 bars.)
Each serving equals:
HE: 1 Br, 3/4 Pr (1/4 limited), 1/4 Fr, 7 OC
175 Calories, 8 gm Fa, 8 gm Pr, 18 gm Ca, 422 mg So
Diabetic: 1 St, 1 Mt, 1 Fa

HINT: Do not use inexpensive rolls. They do not cover
      the pan properly.

JUDY'S CHOCOLATE TOFFEE CRESCENT BARS

1 (8 serving) can Crescent refrigerated rolls
1/4 cup Brown Sugar Twin
1/3 cup reduced calorie margarine
2 oz chopped walnuts (1/2 cup)
4 oz mini chocolate chips (2/3 cup)

Preheat oven to 350 degrees. Pat crescent rolls into ungreased 10x15 jelly roll pan. Gently press dough to cover bottom of pan, being sure to seal perforations. In small saucepan combine Brown Sugar Twin and margarine. Boil 1 minute. Pour mixture evenly over dough. Sprinkle with nuts. Bake 12-16 minutes or until golden brown. Remove from oven, immediately sprinkle with chocolate chips. Slightly swirl pieces as they melt, leaving some pieces partially whole to leave an uneven appearance. Cool on wire rack. Cut into 32 bars.

Serves 16 (2 bars)
Each serving equals:
HE: 3/4 Fa, 1/2 Br, 1/2 Sl, 7 OC
122 Calories, 8 gm Fa, 2 gm Pr, 11 gm Ca, 135 mg So
Diabetic: 1 Fa, 1 St

HINT: Do not use inexpensive rolls. They do not cover
the pan properly.

THIS & THAT

THIS and THAT

BREAKFAST PIZZA

1 (4 serving) can Crescent refrigerated rolls
4 oz fat free cream cheese (1/2 cup)
1/2 teaspoon vanilla extract
2 Tablespoons chunky peanut butter
1 medium banana

Preheat oven to 375 degrees. Spray 9" pie pan with butter flavored cooking spray. Press in crescent rolls. Spread to fill perforations. Bake 10 minutes. Let cool. Mix cream cheese, vanilla extract and peanut butter. Spread mixture over cooled crust. Slice banana and layer on top. Serve at once.

Serves 4
Each serving equals:
HE: 1 Pr, 1 Br, 1/2 Fa, 1/2 Fr
201 Calories, 10 gm Fa, 8 gm Pr, 20 gm Ca, 439 mg So
Diabetic: 1 Mt, 1 St, 1 Fa, 1/2 Fr

APPLESAUCE—OATMEAL MUFFINS

4 1/2 oz uncooked oats (1 1/2 cups)
3/4 cup flour
1/2 teaspoon cinnamon
1 teaspoon baking powder
1/2 teaspoon baking soda
1/4 teaspoon salt
1 cup unsweetened applesauce
1/4 cup skim milk
2 Tablespoons + 2 teaspoons vegetable oil
3 Tablespoons Brown Sugar Twin
1 egg, beaten or equivalent in egg substitute
1/4 cup raisins

Preheat oven to 350 degrees. Spray 12 hole muffin tin with cooking spray. In large bowl combine oats, flour, cinnamon, baking powder, baking soda and salt. Add applesauce, milk, vegetable oil, Brown Sugar Twin, egg and raisins. Fill muffin cups 3/4 full. Bake 20 minutes or until golden brown.

Serves 12
Each serving equals:
HE: 1 Br, 2/3 Fa,1/3 Fr, 9 OC
118 Calories, 3 gm Fa, 3 gm Pr, 19 gm Ca, 114 mg So
Diabetic: 1 St, 1/2 Fr

BLUEBERRY YOGURT MUFFINS

1 1/2 cups flour
1 Tablespoon Sprinkle Sweet
2 Tablespoons Brown Sugar Twin
1 teaspoon baking powder
1/2 teaspoon baking soda
3/4 cup plain fat free yogurt
1 egg, slightly beaten, or equivalent in egg substitute
2 Tablespoons + 2 teaspoons vegetable oil
1 1/2 cups fresh or frozen blueberries,
     thawed and drained

Preheat oven to 425 degrees. Spray 8 hole muffin pan with cooking spray or line with paper baking cups. In large bowl, combine flour, Sprinkle Sweet, Brown Sugar Twin, baking powder and baking soda. Add yogurt, egg and oil. Mix gently just to combine. Fold in blueberries. Fill cups 3/4 full. Bake 20 minutes or until golden brown.

Serves 8
Each serving equals:
HE: 1 Br, 1 Fa, 1/4 Fr, 21 OC
155 Calories, 4 gm Fa, 5 gm Pr, 24 gm Ca, 117 mg So
Diabetic: 1 St, 1 Fa, 1/2 Fr

BAKED POTATO—EGG NESTS

2 teaspoons reduced calorie margarine
1/4 cup chopped onion
1/4 cup chopped green bell pepper
15 oz frozen shredded potatoes,
    slightly thawed (4 cups)
3 oz shredded reduced fat Cheddar cheese (3/4 cup)
1/2 teaspoon salt
1/8 teaspoon lemon pepper
4 eggs or equivalent in egg substitute

Preheat oven to 325 degrees. In large skillet melt margarine. Add onions and green pepper. Saute vegetables until tender-crisp. Stir in potatoes. Cook until potatoes are slightly browned, stirring occasionally. Remove from heat and cool slightly. Stir in 1/2 cup of cheese, salt and pepper. Spoon mixture evenly into 4 individual casseroles sprayed with butter flavored cooking spray. Make an indentation in center of each mixture. Carefully break 1 egg or pour 1/4 of egg substitute into each indentation. Bake 10-20 minutes, depending on desired doneness. Top each with 1 Tablespoon cheese and bake another 2 to 3 minutes.

Serves 4
Each serving equals:
HE: 2 Pr (1 limited), 3/4 Br, 1/4 Ve, 1/4 Fa
221 Calories, 9 gm Fa, 15 gm Pr, 20 gm Ca, 570 mg So
Diabetic: 2 Mt, 1 1/2 St, 1/2 Fa

HINT: Mr. Dell's potatoes work great.

JIFFY EGGS BENEDICT

1 can Campbell's Healthy Request
   Cream of Mushroom soup
3 oz thinly sliced ham (90% lean)
2 English muffins, split, toasted, and lightly
   sprayed with butter flavored cooking spray
4 eggs, poached
1 Tablespoon minced parsley

In medium saucepan heat soup. Spray skillet with butter flavored cooking spray, add ham and brown lightly. Evenly place sliced ham on each muffin half. Top with poached egg. Pour soup over eggs. Sprinkle with minced parsley.

Serves 4
Each serving equals:
HE: 1 3/4 Pr (1 limited), 1 Br, 1/2 Sl, 1 OC
220 Calories, 9 gm Fa, 13 gm Pr, 21 gm Ca, 684 mg So
Diabetic: 2 Mt, 1 1/2 St

HINT: 1) Carl Buddig ham works great.
       2) Egg substitute "Fried" in nonstick skillet sprayed with butter flavored cooking spray can be used in place of eggs.

RODEO OMELET BAKE

2 teaspoons reduced calorie margarine
3 oz diced Dubuque 97% fat free ham (1/2 cup)
1/4 cup chopped green bell pepper
1/4 cup chopped onion
6 eggs, slightly beaten or equivalent in egg substitute
1 can Campbell's Healthy Request
   Cream of Mushroom soup
1/2 cup chunky salsa

Preheat oven to 350 degrees. Melt margarine In large skillet. Add ham, green pepper and onion; saute until crisp tender. Remove from heat. In medium bowl combine eggs and soup. Add slightly cooled ham mixture. Pour into 8 x 8 baking dish, sprayed with butter flavored cooking spray. Place dish inside larger pan that has 1" of water in it. Bake 30 minutes or until done in center. When serving pour 2 Tablespoons salsa sauce over each portion.

Serves 4
Each serving equals:
HE: 2 Pr (1 1/2 limited), 1/2 Ve, 1/4 Fa, 1/2 Sl, 1 OC
187 Calories, 10 gm Fa, 14 gm Pr, 10 gm Ca, 716 mg So
Diabetic: 2 Mt, 2 Ve, 1/2 Fa

WESTERN SCRAMBLE

4 eggs, slightly beaten or equivalent in egg substitute
2 Tablespoons skim milk
1/2 cup canned sliced mushrooms, drained
1/2 teaspoon lemon pepper
2 teaspoons reduced calorie margarine
3 oz diced Dubuque 97% fat free ham (1/2 cup)
1/4 cup chopped green bell pepper
1/4 cup chopped onion
3 oz shredded reduced fat Taco or Cheddar cheese
   (3/4 cup)

In medium bowl combine eggs, skim milk, mushrooms and lemon pepper. In large skillet melt margarine. Add ham, green pepper and onions. Saute until vegetables are tender. Add egg mixture. Cook over low heat until eggs are almost set. Sprinkle top with cheese. Cover for a couple minutes to allow cheese to melt.

Serves 4
Each serving equals:
HE: 2 1/2 Pr(1 limited), 1/2 Ve, 1/4 Fa, 4 OC
163 Calories, 9 gm Fa, 16 gm Pr, 4 gm Ca, 503 mg So
Diabetic: 2 Mt, 1 Free Ve, 1/2 Fa

EGG AND FRANKFURTER SANDWICH FILLING

2 hard boiled eggs, cooled
3.2 oz Healthy Choice 97% fat free frankfurters
1 cup chopped celery
1/4 cup fat free mayonnaise
    (8 calories per Tablespoon)
1/8 teaspoon pepper
1/2 teaspoon dried parsley flakes

Cook and cool frankfurters. Chop eggs and frankfurters into fine pieces and combine in medium bowl. Add celery, mayonnaise, parsley flakes and pepper. Mix well to combine. Chill for 2 hours.

Serves 4 (1/2 cup)
Each serving equals:
HE: 1 Pr, 1/2 Ve, 12 OC
74 Calories, 3 gm Fa, 6 gm Pr, 6 gm Ca, 398 mg So
Diabetic: 1 Mt

HINT: 2 Healthy Choice frankfurters equal 3.2 oz.

SALSA DIP

1 (8 oz) pkg fat free cream cheese
1/4 cup fat free mayonnaise
   (8 calories per Tablespoon)
1 cup chunky salsa

In medium bowl stir cream cheese with spoon until soft. Add mayonnaise. Mix well until light and fluffy. Blend in salsa. Chill at least 2 hours.

Serves 8 (1/4 cup)
Each serving equals:
HE: 1/2 Pr, 1/4 Ve, 4 OC
34 Calories, 0 gm Fa, 4 gm Pr, 4 gm Ca, 349 mg So
Diabetic: 1 Ve

HINT: Good with fresh veggies or crackers.

WHITE HOUSE PUNCH

32 oz low calorie Cranberry Juice Cocktail
16 oz Diet 7-UP

In a large pitcher combine Cranberry Juice Cocktail and Diet 7-UP. Mix well. Serve over ice. Can be doubled and served in a punch bowl with 2 cups ice cubes.

Serves 6 (1 Cup)
Each serving equals:
HE: 2/3 Fr
36 Calories, 0 gm Fa, 0 gm Pr, 9 gm Ca, 16 mg So
Diabetic: 1/2 Fr

My Favorite Recipes

Recipe	Page
Salisbury Steak	115
Rhubarb Fluff Pie	152
(No Time to Cook)	
Grandma's Green Bean Salad	12

My Favorite Recipes

Recipe   Page

_____

_____

_____

_____

_____

_____

_____

_____

_____

_____

_____

_____

_____

_____

_____

_____

_____

INDEX

SOUPS

SALADS

SALADS continued

VEGETABLES

MAIN DISHES

MAIN DISHES continued

DESSERTS

THIS and THAT